# Content-Area
# *Conversations*

How to Plan Discussion-Based Lessons for Diverse Language Learners

# Content-Area
# Conversations

How to Plan Discussion-Based Lessons for Diverse Language Learners

## Douglas Fisher | Nancy Frey | Carol Rothenberg

Association for Supervision and Curriculum Development
Alexandria, Virginia USA

Association for Supervision and Curriculum Development
1703 N. Beauregard St. • Alexandria, VA 22311-1714 USA
Phone: 800-933-2723 or 703-578-9600 • Fax: 703-575-5400
Web site: www.ascd.org • E-mail: member@ascd.org
Author guidelines: www.ascd.org/write

Gene R. Carter, *Executive Director;* Nancy Modrak, *Publisher;* Julie Houtz, *Director of Book Editing & Production;* Ernesto Yermoli, *Project Manager;* Cathy Guyer, *Senior Graphic Designer;* Mike Kalyan, *Production Manager;* BMWW, *Typesetter;* Carmen Yuhas, *Production Specialist*

All Web links in this book are correct as of the publication date below but may have become inactive or otherwise modified since that time. If you notice a deactivated or changed link, please e-mail books@ascd.org with the words "Link Update" in the subject line. In your message, please specify the Web link, the book title, and the page number on which the link appears.

PAPERBACK ISBN: 978-1-4166-0737-3      ASCD product #108035   s10/08
Also available as an e-book through ebrary, netLibrary, and many online booksellers (see Books in Print for the ISBNs).

Quantity discounts for the paperback edition only: 10–49 copies, 10%; 50+ copies, 15%; for 1,000 or more copies, call 800-933-2723, ext. 5634, or 703-575-5634. For desk copies: member@ascd.org.

Library of Congress Cataloging-in-Publication Data

Fisher, Douglas, 1965–
  Content-area conversations : how to plan discussion-based lessons for diverse language learners / Douglas Fisher, Carol Rothenberg, and Nancy Frey.
     p. cm.
  Includes bibliographical references and index.
     ISBN 978-1-4166-0737-3 (pbk. : alk. paper)   1. English language—Study and teaching—Foreign speakers.   2. Language arts—Correlation with content subjects.
3. Discussion.   I. Rothenberg, Carol.   II. Frey, Nancy, 1959–   III. Title.

  PE1128.A2F542 2008
  428.0071—dc22
                                                                                    2008028766

18 17 16 15 14 13 12 11 10 09 08      1 2 3 4 5 6 7 8 9 10 11 12

*In loving memory of
Harriet Rothenberg—mother, teacher,
counselor, attorney, inspiration*

# Content-Area Conversations

## How to Plan Discussion-Based Lessons for Diverse Language Learners

# Foreword

Virginia Woolf's 1938 book of essays, *Three Guineas,* opens with a letter to a barrister who has asked the question, "How are we to prevent war?" The question leads Woolf to weave throughout her answer a theme that must have seemed odd, if not irrelevant, to readers of the time: the work of language in the academy. In writing to the barrister, Woolf speaks for and through the voices of women, the poor, and other groups excluded from the academy while also holding out the ideal purpose of advanced learning—to address eternally vexing questions.

Woolf despairs that the academy will never be inclusive or take up society's hardest questions. She points out that while the academy remains inert, society and the needs of all its citizens continue to change. How must universities tackle the real, practical need to teach students to earn their living while also presenting them with the wisdom of the masters? If trained to teach, can instructors use their influence to address questions such as how to prevent war? Or must the educated, in the end, merely maintain the status quo? Must the university rely so heavily on lectures and examinations and undertake only research that promises to yield monetary rewards? Woolf calls on "the face on the other side of the page" to recognize that the educated often come to focus their energies on acquiring possessions and gaining power; various forms of force become their accepted means of moving forward. In the end, Woolf argues, the university must be "rebuilt" and education must be altered (1938, p. 35).

Woolf's letter contains within it an imagined response to itself, invoking the dialogic and deliberative nature of what has come to be called "academic language." Those from the academy always assume a knowing, conversing audience; indeed, the academic essay traces its roots to conversation. English essayists such as Francis Bacon, Charles Lamb, and Virginia Woolf made dialogue and a give-and-take of ideas the essence of their essays on social values, habits, and arts (Heath, 1993, 1997). Woolf's letter to the barrister continues this dialogue through artful persuasion as well as strong argumentation with claims, warrants, and evidence. In demonstrating these fundamentals of academic language, Woolf gives her readers a look at the give-and-take of substantive conversation among the "informed."

The book you hold in your hands echoes Woolf's affirmation of talk as fundamental to learning. Good conversation among individuals who care and are informed about a topic provides the groundwork for reading and writing as well as listening intently and carefully to deliberation. Though this volume focuses on the importance of talk in classrooms, I extend the claims made for this situation to other settings—intimate get-togethers with family or friends, for example, or casual conversations with new acquaintances in informal public settings. The more frequently we engage in deliberation, the greater the ease with which we raise a narrative as point of evidence within an argument. (Consider, for example, the importance of narrative in legal testimony and argumentation.) The more extended the opportunities for talk, the more fluid the speaker's flow of evidence and reference points.

The reality is that the practice time available in classrooms is not sufficient to build fluency in students who have few other occasions for extended conversation on weighty topics. The harsh truth is that listening and multiparty talk occur too rarely in classrooms. The authors of this book have good reason to question higher education's need to continue its dependence on lecture and examinations.

*Content-Area Conversations* helps learners to understand some fundamentals of rhetoric, such as deliberative discourse (one of Aristotle's three types of rhetoric, along with forensic and epideictic). Repeatedly addressed since the 1990s by political scientists and philosophers, such discourse is often referred to in the context of "deliberative democracy" and generally refers to deliberation that centers on political considerations (Mutz, 2006). Distinct from debate in that two oppositional positions are not assumed, deliberative discourse gives voice to multiple positions and views, centers on the common good or democratic values, and brings new information and perspectives into the open in a collaborative spirit. Critical to deliberative discourse is the fact that the process takes precedence over the status of participants; a central authority does not power over conclusions or pronouncements regarding consensus. Such discourse is therefore often paired with the descriptor *participatory.*

This volume also presents core ideas from linguistics, such as *register,* that call attention to roles and what lies behind these roles in terms of representation. Learners only begin to make connections among experiences when they feel that what is to be learned has value and meaning—a notion reinforced in the section on different conversational norms of English language learners and the importance of strategies of inclusion. Throughout the book, we learn ways to help learners gain a curiosity and fascination with language and grasp the meaning of "metalanguage."

Chapter 6 addresses a central irony of the contemporary climate of assessment. Though educators frequently use terms such as *accountability, evaluation,* and *standards,* rarely do they consider the best ways to assess the most frequent means of communication among the young: oral language, visual media, and performance. This volume shows how teachers can use multiple means of assessment and establish opportunities to model language and offer meaningful situations of oral language exchange. The teachers whose words, ways, and wisdom are discussed in this book represent exceptional caring, connecting, and communicating. Their patterns of listening, talking, researching, and inquiring are not routine classroom *practices*; rather, they represent the deep *principles* that shape roles and relationships.

"Academic language" consists not of lectures, examinations, force, or avoidance of questions that cry out for deliberation. Quite the opposite: true academic language lies in the details of vocabulary,

syntax, and genres that characterize deliberative, democratic participation across roles and responsibilities. If we were to analyze the
linguistic structures most frequently illustrated in this volume, we
would find numerous "rare words" with clear definitions and examples worked into conversations by the teachers. We would also find
open-ended questions, hypotheticals, "if–then" propositions, narra-
tives of argumentation, and mental-state verbs that ask students to
imagine, plan, think about, wonder, and speculate. These linguistic
structures are the nuts and bolts within deliberative discourse that
set learners on their way to taking in information as well as determining the bases, merits, and possibilities of that information.

Of course, learning about language goes well beyond the classroom. If classrooms become havens of extensive deliberative talk, we
can depend on the joy and exhilaration of such participation to spill
into other participatory occasions. We need to ensure that our learning is *lifelong, life-wide,* and *life-deep* (Banks et al., 2007).

Lifelong learning depends on our acquiring attitudes, fundamental behaviors, and real-world information that enable us to keep on
learning. Thus, we fare best in life if we have opportunities very early
to hear and use language that will shape our pursuit of curiosity
("But what happens when that's not there?"), enable us to challenge
and test ideas ("Does that mean there's only one way to get that
answer?"), and persist in collaborative ventures ("We're trying to
work it out, but we've got to help each other with this vocabulary").
Through using such language, we develop the mental habit of self-
assessment as well as the capacity to observe and listen to what is
happening with others around us. We learn to ask hard questions of
ourselves and others. Such habits of language—if started early—stay
long with us.

The width of our lives is determined by the range of experiences
we have and the extent of empathic reasoning we master. Life-wide
learning comes through experience managing our learning with and
from others across time, space, and unexpected turns of events. We
have to figure out how to adapt, transport knowledge and skills from
one situation to another, and transform direct experience into tactics

and strategies for the future. To gain life-wide learning, we need opportunities to play an array of roles and take up multiple responsibilities with the help of caring scaffolding and strong modeling. Early experiences in life-wide learning ensure that we learn to see others' points of view, sense the experience of how others live, and know why is it important to think anew about questions such as how to prevent war and how to remake education.

Life-deep learning is the hardest to develop. Before writing *Three Guineas,* Virginia Woolf and her husband, Leonard, had visited Italy and experienced fascism up close. Throughout the late 1930s, news of Germany and its impending invasion of Great Britain was constant in their lives. The fate of Jews, the indifference of nations, and the persistence of war were at once intensely private (Leonard was Jewish) and public for them. Their writings and activities tell of their sense of the pain of others and their attempts to speak for the silenced and expose the torturing effects of oppression. Virginia, in particular, pled that education be available and accessible without regard for gender, class, or birthright. Life-deep learning encompasses our commitment to religious, moral, spiritual, and ethical values in relation to our behavior and social relationships. We create this deep learning as we develop and examine our beliefs, ideologies, and orientations to facing life with integrity and respect for self and others.

In the end, academic language is not just academic. It is life giving when it extends through the length, width, and depth of all that we can learn. Such language allows us to question, deliberate, negotiate, ponder, and imagine. Fluency and ease in this kind of talk help us to find our way in the world and humanity to make the world a better place.

—*Shirley Brice Heath*

# Introduction

A s so often happens when writing a book, we encountered a new study along the way that echoed many of the concerns we were writing about. The Longitudinal Immigrant Student Adaptation Study, led by Carola and Marcelo Suárez-Oroczo and Irina Todorova (2008), followed the academic and personal lives of more than 400 new arrivals to the United States for five years as they moved through middle and high school. Their findings were predictable to any who have dedicated their professional lives to these most hopeful students: that proficiency in English was the best predictor of academic achievement. This is no surprise considering that our measures of academic achievement are overwhelmingly in English. Sadly, over the course of the five-year study, more than two-thirds of the participants saw their grade point averages (GPAs) steadily decline.

This study resonated with us for other reasons as well. The researchers found that social engagement with teachers and peers, as well as students' cognitive inquisitiveness, played a significant role (30 percent of the variance in GPA) in achievement. The good news is that we as teachers have the means to promote the mental and relational connections necessary for learning. Our most effective tool is the talk we foster in our classrooms. We're not referring to the social chatter of peers making plans for after school (it seems as though that blossoms almost without our help!), nor do we mean the sound of our own voices filling the air. We mean the learning discourse—the back-and-forth discussion of ideas that deepens understanding.

Jeff Zwiers's (2007) careful study of the practices that enhance and inhibit discourse is a reminder of how the best of intentions are undermined when misapplied. We should use questioning to provoke thought, but that should not be mistaken for the interrogative practices that ask for little more than recall (Doug calls these practices "guess what's in the teacher's brain"). The use of gestures to reinforce the meaning of terminology is helpful, but not if it is so culturally bound that its meaning is lost. Zwiers cites the example of a teacher who flashed a peace sign with her fingers when she used the term *pacify*—a reference lost to many of her middle school English language learners. Most dishearteningly, he found that teachers too often accepted insufficient responses in a misguided effort to reduce the pressure on English language learners. Call it the "soft bigotry of low expectations," if you will (politicians on both sides of the aisle have done so), but a willingness to accept less and expect less from students who are learning English while learning *in* English communicates a lack of faith in their ability.

Of course, this doesn't mean ignoring the needs of students by wrapping ourselves in a cloak of "high standards for all." It *does* mean approaching academic discourse in our classrooms with the same precision that we devote to the content. We have written this book to describe the framework we use in our own teaching to foster the kind of talk that leads to the development of academic learning necessary for students to succeed:

- *Planning for purposeful talk* by incorporating standards; establishing a clear purpose; and identifying learning, language, and social objectives for lessons
- *Creating an environment* that encourages academic discourse, including the physical room arrangement, teaching the routines of talk, and scaffolding language
- *Managing the academic discourse* through grouping and collaborative activities that increase confidence and provide students with ways to consolidate learning with peers
- *Assessing academic language development* using practical tools for monitoring progress and identifying areas of need

We hope you find this framework useful in your own practice. Our task as educators is a huge one: to meet the diverse needs of learners, adhere to high expectations, and develop our students' sense of self as productive and valued citizens. To us, it all comes back to language. When we equip our learners with the tools to explain, inquire, question, dispute, and elaborate, we realize each of these missions.

# Why Talk Is
# Important in Classrooms

Aldous Huxley (1958) once wrote, "Language has made possible man's progress from animality to civilization" (p. 167). In doing so, he effectively summarized the importance of language in humans' lives. It is through language that we are civilized. One could argue that nothing is more important to the human species than that. But Huxley wasn't done there; he continued by explaining the value of language:

> Language permits its users to pay attention to things, persons and events, even when the things and persons are absent and the events are not taking place. Language gives definition to our memories and, by translating experiences into symbols, converts the immediacy of craving or abhorrence, or hatred or love, into fixed principles of feeling and conduct. (p. 168)

Language, in other words, is how we think. It's how we process information and remember. It's our operating system. Vygotsky (1962) suggested that thinking develops into words in a number of phases, moving from imaging to inner speech to inner speaking to speech. Tracing this idea backward, speech—talk—is the representation of thinking. As such, it seems reasonable to suggest that classrooms should be filled with talk, given that we want them filled with thinking!

## A Brief History of Classroom Talk

Academic discourse has always been part of the classroom. Teachers have long understood the importance of using language to transmit ideas. In the early history of education, teachers talked for most of the instructional day while students were quiet and completed their assigned tasks. Students were expected to memorize facts and be able to recite them. Remember that in most classrooms of the late 1800s, the age range was very diverse. In the same classroom, teachers might have students who were 5 or 6 years old and others who were 15 to 18. Talking by students was not the norm. In fact, students were punished for talking in class, even if the talk was academic!

Over time, educators realized that students had to use the language if they were to become better educated. As a result, well-intentioned educators called on individual students to respond to questions. Teachers expected them to use academic language in their individual responses, and as students spoke, teachers would assess their knowledge. Consider the following exchange from a 3rd grade class. As you read it, think about how much academic language was used:

**Teacher:** I was thinking about the life cycle of an insect. Do you remember the life cycle we studied? Malik?

**Malik:** Yes.

**Teacher:** What was the first stage in the life cycle? Jesse?

**Jesse:** They was born?

**Teacher:** Yes, things are born, but think about the life cycle of insects. Let's try to be more specific in our thinking. What is the first stage in the insect life cycle? Miriam?

**Miriam:** Eggs.

**Teacher:** Yes, insects start as eggs. Then they change and develop. They become larva after eggs, right? And then what? What happens to them after they are larva? Adrian?

**Adrian:** They are adults.

**Teacher:** They do eventually become adults, but there is a step missing. What is the step between larva and adults? What is that stage of the life cycle called? Joe?

**Joe:** Mature larva?

**Teacher:** Yes, there are two kinds of larva in the life cycle of some insects. But what I was thinking about was what happened to them after the larva before they become adults. Mariah?

**Mariah:** Nymph?

**Teacher:** Now we're talking about the three-stage cycle for some insects. Do the insects that change into nymphs come from larva? Let's look at our two posters again. Remember these? There is a three-stage process and a four-stage process. Let's study these again.

Let's spend a few minutes analyzing this classroom exchange. First, it's not unlike many of the whole-class interactions we've seen, especially in a classroom where the students are obviously having a difficult time with the content. One student at a time is talking while the others listen or ignore the class. Second, the teacher is clearly using a lot of academic language, which is great. We know that teachers themselves have to use academic discourse if their students are ever going to have a chance to learn. Third, the balance of talk in this classroom is heavily weighted toward the teacher. If we count the number of words used, minus the student names, the teacher used 190 words, whereas the students used 11. This means that 94 percent of the words used in the classroom during this five-minute segment were spoken by the teacher. In addition, if we analyze the types of words used, half of the words spoken by the students were not academic in nature. That's not so great. Students need more time to talk, and this structure of asking them to do so one at a time will not significantly change the balance of talk in the classroom.

As you reflect on this excerpt from the classroom, consider whether you think that the students will ever become proficient in using the language. Our experience suggests that these students will fail to develop academic language and discourse simply because they aren't provided opportunities to use words. They are hearing words but are not using them. We are reminded of Bakhtin's (1981) realization: "The world in language is half someone else's. It becomes 'one's own' only when the speaker populates it with his own intention, his own accent, when he appropriates the word, adapting it to his own semantic and expressive intention" (pp. 293–294). In other words, if students aren't using the words, they aren't developing academic discourse. As a result, we often think we've done a remarkable job teaching students and then wonder why they aren't learning. The key is for students to talk with one another, in purposeful ways, using academic language. Let's explore the importance of talk as the foundation for literacy next.

## Talk: Building the Foundation for Literacy

Wilkinson (1965) introduced the term *oracy* as a way for people to think about the role that oral language plays in literacy development, defining it as "the ability to express oneself coherently and to communicate freely with others by word of mouth." Wilkinson noted that the development of oracy would lead to increased skill in reading and writing as users of the language became increasingly proficient—as James Britton (1983) put it so eloquently, "Reading and writing float on a sea of talk" (p. 11).

Put simply, talk, or oracy, is the foundation of literacy. This should not come as a surprise to anyone. We have all observed that young children listen and speak well before they can read or write. Children learn to manipulate their environment with spoken words well before they learn to do so with written words. It seems that this pattern is developmental in nature and that our brains are wired for language. Young children learn that language is power and that they can use words to express their needs, wants, and desires.

The problem with applying this developmental approach to English language learners and language learning in the classroom is that our students don't have years to learn to speak before they need to write. Historically, teachers did not introduce English language learners to print until they had developed their speaking skills—a misguided approach that does not take into account the fact that, in developing their primary language, English language learners have already learned much about language, including the role that it plays in interacting with others. At the other end of the spectrum of instructional practice, many teachers did not provide any oral language instruction because they believed that their students needed to develop reading proficiency (and make adequate yearly progress) as soon as possible.

Instead of this either/or approach, English language learners need access to instruction that recognizes the symbiotic relationship among the four domains of language: listening, speaking, reading, and writing. Clearly, students must reach high levels of proficiency in reading and writing in order to be successful in school, at a university, and in virtually any career they may choose. We know that it takes time to reach those levels. We know that opportunities for students to talk in class also take time. So, given the little instructional time we have with them, how can we justify devoting a significant amount of that time to talk? We would argue, How can we *not* provide that time to talk? *Telling* students what you want them to know is certainly a faster way of addressing standards. But *telling* does not necessarily equate to *learning.* If indeed "reading and writing float on a sea of talk," then the time students spend engaged in academic conversations with their classmates is time well spent in developing not only oracy but precisely the high level of literacy that is our goal. In Chapter 3 we will explore how we can maximize use of instructional time to that end.

## Talk in the Average Classroom

Classroom talk is frequently limited and is used to check comprehension rather than develop thinking. Consistent with the example from the beginning of the chapter, researchers have found that teachers dominate classroom talk. For example, Lingard, Hayes, and Mills

(2003) noted that in classrooms with higher numbers of students living in poverty, teachers talk more and students talk less. We also know that English language learners in many classrooms are asked easier questions or no questions at all and thus rarely have to talk in the classroom (Guan Eng Ho, 2005). Several decades ago, Flanders (1970) reported that teachers of high-achieving students spent about 55 percent of the class time talking, compared with 80 percent for teachers of low-achieving students.

In addition to the sheer volume of teacher talk in the classroom, researchers have identified the types of talk that are more and less helpful. For example, Durkin's (1978/1979) seminal research on comprehension instruction confirmed that teachers rely primarily on questioning to check for understanding. Questioning is an important tool that teachers have, but students also need opportunities for dialogue if they are to learn. And, unfortunately, most questioning uses an initiate–respond–evaluate cycle (Cazden, 1988) in which teachers initiate a question, a student responds, and then the teacher evaluates the answer. Here is an example from a 7th grade social studies discussion of a reading on ancient Mesopotamia:

**Teacher:** What did the Sumerians use to control the Twin Rivers? (*initiate*)

**Justin:** Levees? (*respond*)

**Teacher:** Right. (*evaluate*) And why did the Sumerians want to control the Twin Rivers? (*initiate, again*)

The problems inherent in this type of approach are multiple. First, in a classroom where we want students to talk—to practice and apply their developing knowledge of English—only one student has an opportunity to talk, and, as we see in this example, that talk does not require the use of even one complete sentence, let alone extended discourse. In a classroom where we want students to analyze, synthesize, and evaluate, neither does this type of interchange require them to engage in critical thinking. Instead, they may become frustrated as they struggle to "guess what's in the teacher's head" or become disengaged as they listen to the "popcorn" pattern of teacher question, student response, teacher question, student response, and so on. Last, in a classroom where assessment guides instruction, with each question the teacher learns that one student knows the answer but can make no determination regarding the understanding of the other 29 students in the classroom.

In sum, talk is used in most classrooms but could be more effectively used to develop students' thinking. Teachers must take into account their English language learners' current proficiency levels when planning instruction.

## Differences Among Students

One of the most important things to recognize about teaching English language learners is that they are not a monolithic group. They differ in a number of important ways, including the following:

**Linguistic.** Although Spanish is the most common second language in the United States, students in a given school district might speak more than 100 different languages. These languages differ in their pronunciation patterns, orthographic representations, and histories—and thus in the ease with which students can transfer their prior knowledge about language to English.

**Proficiency in the home language.** Students who speak the same language and are in the same grade may have very different levels of academic language proficiency in their home language depending on such factors as age and prior education. The development of a formal first language facilitates learning in additional languages.

**Generation.** There are recognized differences in language proficiency for students of different generations living in the United States. First and second generations of English language learners differ in significant ways, including the ability to use English at home. Because protracted English language learners born outside the United States attempt to straddle their old world and the new world in which they live, they experience greater difficulty in developing English proficiency.

**Number of languages spoken.** Some students enroll in schools having mastered more than one language already and thus have gained a linguistic flexibility that can aid in learning additional languages. Others have spoken one language at home for years, and their exposure to English is a new learning experience.

**Motivation.** Students differ in their motivation to learn English depending on their migration, immigration, or birthplace. Immigrant families leave their homelands for a variety of reasons—political and economic are perhaps the most common. Many of our students have left loved ones behind, along with a familiar and cherished way of life. Some even hope to return when a war is ended or when the family has enough money to better their life in their home country. These students may not feel a great need to become proficient in a language they don't intend to use for very long.

**Poverty.** Living in poverty and experiencing food insecurity have a profound impact on learning in general and language learning in particular. Simply said, when students' basic needs are met, they are more likely to excel in school.

**Personality.** Some students are naturally outgoing and verbal; others are shy or prefer more independent activities. Some are risk takers who are not afraid to make mistakes; others want their utterances to be perfect. These differences in personality can lead to differences in the rate at which students gain proficiency in listening and speaking or reading and writing.

## Levels of Proficiency

Having acknowledged various differences among students, we also recognize the need to cluster them into levels of proficiency for instructional purposes. There are a number of ways to do this, but we have chosen the Teachers of English to Speakers of Other Languages (TESOL) levels: Starting, Emerging, Developing, Expanding, and Bridging (TESOL, 2006). Figure 1.1 provides an overview of each of these proficiency levels, and they are summarized here as well:

**Figure 1.1    Performance Definitions of the Five Levels of English Language Proficiency**

English language learners can understand and use …

| Level 1 Starting | Level 2 Emerging | Level 3 Developing | Level 4 Expanding | Level 5 Bridging |
|---|---|---|---|---|
| … language to communicate with others around basic concrete needs. | … language to draw on simple and routine experiences to communicate with others. | … language to communicate with others on familiar matters regularly encountered. | … language in both concrete and abstract situations and apply language to new experiences. | … a wide range of longer oral and written texts and recognize implicit meaning. |
| … high-frequency words and memorized chunks of language. | … high-frequency and some general academic vocabulary and expressions. | … general and some specialized academic vocabulary and expressions. | … specialized and some technical academic vocabulary and expressions. | … technical academic vocabulary and expressions. |
| … words, phrases, or chunks of language. | … phrases or short sentences in oral or written communication. | … expanded sentences in oral or written communication. | … a variety of sentence lengths of varying linguistic complexity in oral and written communication. | … a variety of sentence lengths of varying linguistic complexity in extended oral or written discourse. |
| … pictorial, graphic, or nonverbal representation of language. | … oral or written language, making errors that often impede the meaning of the communication. | … oral or written language, making errors that may impede the communication but retain much of its meaning. | … oral or written language, making minimal errors that do not impede the overall meaning of the communication. | … oral or written language approaching comparability to that of English-proficient peers. |

*Source:* TESOL (2006), *PreK–12 English Language Proficiency Standards: Augmentation of the World-Class Instructional Design and Assessment (WIDA) Consortium English Language Proficiency Standards* (Alexandria, VA: Author), p. 39. Used with permission.

**Starting.** At this entry level, students have virtually no understanding of English and do not use English to communicate. They might respond to simple commands or questions, often nonverbally. Over time, they begin to imitate the oral language of those around them and will speak in one-word responses. Reading in English is very difficult, but students might recognize sight words or words that are similar to those in their home language. Pictorial representations are helpful, as are physical responses. When students who are starting to learn English write, they exhibit a number of unconventional spellings and grammatical errors.

**Emerging.** As students are introduced to academic English appropriate for their age, their language emerges. Students at this level begin to understand phrases and simple sentences. They begin to communicate their needs, wants, and desires, especially using familiar and often memorized phrases or word groupings. In addition, they begin to speak in sentences but often make syntax errors in doing so. When they read and write in English, they can recognize familiar and high-frequency words. They can also copy information but make errors in grammar that interfere with effective communication.

**Developing.** During this phase, students add considerably to their vocabulary. They use English spontaneously and are generally understood but often experience difficulty expressing feelings and other abstract ideas and continue to make grammar errors. As a group, they continue to produce simple sentences but understand sentences that are much more complex. They read increasingly complex texts and write more coherent information. Although their writing typically contains a number of errors and nonconventional forms, students in this place are able to demonstrate their thinking and understanding of the tasks at hand.

**Expanding.** At this level, students' language skills are sufficient for most daily communication tasks. Although they make occasional structural errors, the majority of their communication is clear. They participate in discussions and use English in unfamiliar settings, though idioms and other figurative language forms may present a challenge. Generally, students at this level can read well enough to gain information from a text and write fairly independently; however, their writing is typically scored below grade level because they use less sophisticated text structures and vocabulary.

**Bridging.** At this advanced level of proficiency, students generally perform well across the language domains of speaking, listening, reading, and writing. Their speech becomes increasingly fluent, and they can discuss a variety of topics with ease. They can do grade-level work but may need some guidance for technical writing and reading.

After considering each of these proficiency levels, it's easy to see the importance of talking. At each level, the development of oral language is related to developing skills in written language. Equally important is the fact that reading and writing are not deferred while speech develops; rather, students are reading, writing, speaking, and listening from the beginning of their introduction into English. In addition, these English language learners are wrestling with what they know and do not know regarding language functions and registers, both of which are informed by the context of the discourse— mode, topic, purpose, audience, setting, and so forth.

## When Talk Facilitates Learning

Figure 1.2 provides a graphic representation of the opportunities for integrating talk in the classroom. We've divided the opportunities for talk into four major categories. These categories are consistent with a gradual release of responsibility model of instruction, which acknowledges that students must assume increasing responsibility if they are to learn (Fisher & Frey, 2008). This does not mean that students are supposed to become independent learners in the absence of the teacher but, rather, that classrooms are structured in such a way that students are introduced to ideas and then have opportunities to work with these ideas before being expected to complete tasks independently. As you'll see throughout this book, a number of instructional strategies are available for integrating purposeful student talk. For

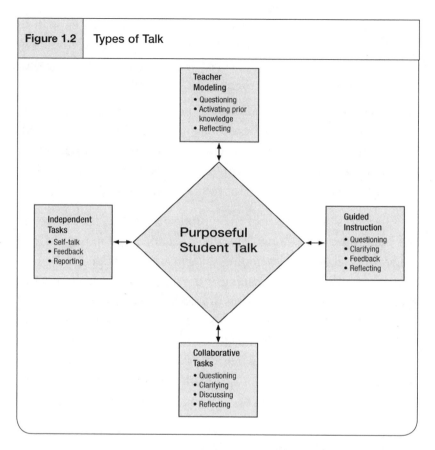

| Figure 1.2 | Types of Talk |

**Teacher Modeling**
- Questioning
- Activating prior knowledge
- Reflecting

**Independent Tasks**
- Self-talk
- Feedback
- Reporting

**Purposeful Student Talk**

**Guided Instruction**
- Questioning
- Clarifying
- Feedback
- Reflecting

**Collaborative Tasks**
- Questioning
- Clarifying
- Discussing
- Reflecting

now, let's consider the instructional routines in which talk can be integrated.

## Teacher Modeling

During whole-class instruction, teachers model behaviors, skills, and strategies that they expect to see from their students. As we will discuss in Chapter 3, this modeling is based on an established purpose and provides students with a mental model for completing tasks they will encounter in another phase of instruction. We've already seen that questioning can be used during teacher modeling, but teachers can also activate their students' background knowledge during this time (for example, a 10th grade biology teacher might ask his students to talk with a partner about cell life before he explains cell division to them). In addition, teachers model the use of academic language as they engage in think alouds, shared readings, read alouds, lectures, and other whole-class events. After modeling, students can reflect on what they learned through both writing independently and talking with a partner.

## Guided Instruction

During guided instructional events, teachers use talk to determine what students know and what they still need to know. This is an opportunity to use questions, prompts, and cues to help students complete tasks. Although guided instruction is teacher led, this does not mean that students are not talking. They use talk to ask questions—of the teacher, of peers, and of themselves—as well as to clarify understanding, provide feedback to a partner, and reflect once more on their learning.

As we will see in subsequent chapters, teachers can use talk during guided instruction in a number of ways. For example, an art teacher might meet with a small group of students who have difficulty with perspective in their drawings. He asks them to compare and contrast several drawings from his collections of books and then has them give one-word explanations of the differences. The students use words such as *proportion, line,* and *shading.* Through talk, this art teacher is able to facilitate increased understanding for his students.

## Collaborative Tasks

In this phase of instruction, students are provided an opportunity to work together, with the teacher monitoring and supporting as needed. Talk becomes critical when students discuss tasks or ideas and question one another, negotiate meaning, clarify their own understanding, and make their ideas comprehensible to their partners. It is during collaborative tasks that students must use academic language if they are to focus on the content. Here again, their understanding grows as they talk with their partners to reflect on their learning. A number of classroom structures, such as reciprocal teaching, literature circles, partner discussions, and so on, require students to talk together. Our experience suggests that this phase of instruction is critical for English language learners to use the language and, as Bakhtin noted, own the words and ideas.

### Independent Tasks

It might seem strange to suggest that talk plays a critical role during independent activities. But think about the self-talk (inner speaking) you use when you complete independent tasks. Some of this self-talk occurs in your mind, whereas some is vocalized. Again, thinking occurs as we use language, and this type of talk is an important aspect to learning. As students work independently, they may also use talk to receive input on their work and give feedback to others. Reporting out after independent work may require a more formal register of language than that used during collaborative activities.

As an example of the type of instruction in which talk permeates the learning environment, let us peek inside a 5th grade classroom as students read and discuss *Hattie Big Sky* (Larson, 2006). The teacher has just finished reading a chapter aloud. As she was reading, she regularly paused to provide context clues for vocabulary words. For example, when she came to the word *skyscraper*, she paused and commented, "What a great word! I know from the context that it's a type of building, but I can really see this in my mind. The big tall buildings in Chicago must have seemed to really scrape the sky. Have you seen buildings like that? Describe a skyscraper to your partner."

At that moment, the classroom bursts into talk. Teresa leans over to Javier and says, "Like totally covered in glass, you know, all shiny so that you can see yourself. It's so big, you can see the ocean when you're up there."

After the reading and think aloud, the teacher asks students to think about the differences in life in San Diego today and Montana in 1918. She says, "There are two things on my mind that we should talk about. There are differences and similarities between San Diego and the town Hattie lives in: Vida, Montana. And there are also differences and similarities between today and 1918. Choose one of those topics to discuss with your partner."

Pedro turns to Alex and says, "They had nice people and mean people, just like we do. But they got bad weather and we don't." Alex responds, "Yeah, and they have farms and we don't, but they have chores like we do."

Following the whole-class and partner discussions, students moved to their collaborative learning groups. The teacher had purposefully organized the membership in these groups such that students at the beginning levels of English proficiency had access to language brokers who could support their participation. She also focused on creating groups with diverse interests and skill levels such that the group would become interdependent as they processed information.

One of the collaborative learning tasks required students to create a readers' theater script based on the chapter they had read. Their teacher knows that students will reread the text, talk about it, practice reading the scripts, and provide one another feedback on their speaking parts as a component of this task. A few lines from the script written by Alex's group highlight the ways in which language and talk are used to facilitate learning:

**Hattie:** I gotta get my chores done but I'm so cold.

**Narrator:** What will I do? I don't want to freeze to death.

**Hattie:** I put on all of my clothes at once, every stitch. That will help me face the extreme cold.

**Mr. Whiskers:** I'm not going outside with you—you're crazy! But there might be milk. I guess I'll go.

**Narrator:** The cow was waiting so Hattie braved the weather.

**Rooster Jim:** Howdy neighbor.

**Hattie:** Oh, hello. Do you want some coffee? I'm almost done and could use some company.

The class continued on with productive group work and all of the talk associated with it. In this classroom, the teacher and her students share the responsibility for talking. Importantly, not just one student talks at a time; during partner conversations, 50 percent of the students are talking at a time. The important thing to remember is that this talk has to be purposeful; it can't just be social if we are going to see improvements in achievement.

## Summary

As we analyze why many students are not learning what we are teaching, we must evaluate our own practice for evidence of student talk throughout the day. Oral language is the foundation of literacy, and as such, it requires focused attention in planning. Altering the ratio of teacher to student talk doesn't just happen. Rather, it occurs through both believing in the importance of student talk and planning with a clear purpose and expectations. But before we discuss *how* to plan lessons that integrate purposeful academic talk, reading, and writing, we must be clear on our own understanding of exactly *what* academic oral discourse is. We turn our attention now to an analysis of the elements of discourse in the classroom.

# Fostering
# Academic Discourse

*There is more than a verbal tie between the words* common, community, *and* communication. . . . *Try the experiment of communicating, with fullness and accuracy, some experience to another, especially if it be somewhat complicated, and you will find your own attitude toward your experience changing.*

—John Dewey (1916, pp. 5–6)

Dewey's elegant description of the power of discourse—reasoning through conversation, argument, or explanation—describes a phenomenon we have all lived: the clarification of one's understanding in the midst of sharing an idea with another. Students in classrooms alive with the rich talk of learning also experience this as they communicate with one another.

All living things communicate. Biologically speaking, communication is the way in which one organism acts upon another. In the living world around us, we witness communication daily as we hear birds sing, watch two dogs greet one another in an elaborate sniffing ceremony, or see fish in an aquarium change colors as they warily approach one another. As humans, we use similar communication skills to announce our presence, to greet another, or to warn someone away.

For communication to take place, there must be two players: a transmitter and a receiver. In the middle is the message, which is transmitted in a variety of ways, including nonverbally (facial expressions, gestures), through paralanguage (pitch, rate, and volume), and within a particular form (oral or written). The variables associated with the type and form used by the sender always result in a difference in understanding by the receiver. Most often, the two players are closely aligned so that the message is shared and understood well enough. However, disasters large and small are sure to erupt when there is a mismatch. This mismatch is exacerbated when either or both participants are learning English while simultaneously learning *in* English.

Our explanation of communication is simplistic because communication is not only a biological function but also a social construct, and the nuances of effective communication vary from one culture to another. In addition, personal experiences, social class, and background knowledge influence communicators. Before we delve into strategies for supporting English language learners, we must have an understanding of the characteristics of discourse across languages. By understanding these commonalities, we can draw upon what our English language learners already know about communication.

## What Is Academic Discourse?

Although all animals communicate, humans possess unique abilities as they relate to oral and written forms. We use extended oral and written messages to reason with other humans. These sophisticated messages, called *discourse*, are further characterized by their form and content. Forms of discourse include explanation, elaboration, evaluation, argument, and questioning. Graff and Birkenstein (2006) call this "entering a conversation of ideas" (p. ix), and it remains a challenge in any classroom, at any level. No form of discourse can exist without the presence of and interaction with another human. Explanation is purposeless if there is no one in need of the information; evaluation is pointless if there isn't someone else who will agree and disagree. Stated simply, a student cannot learn cognitive structures of thought without opportunities to apply them with others.

The academic discourse of the classroom, both oral and written, is the conduit for learning. Written discourse is formalized through the rhetorical writing structures many of us remember from college:

- *Ethos*—a written appeal based on the character of the author
- *Pathos*—a written persuasion based on emotion
- *Logos*—a written appeal based on logical argument and reasoning

We don't teach younger students using this formalized language, but we do instruct them on the common forms of writing, including personal narrative, description, persuasive and expository writing, and the rhetorical styles and devices typically used in each of those genres.

Students should also be instructed on the discourse of classroom learning. In the best learning environments, this happens through *dialogic instruction* (Nystrand, 1997)—that is, a teacher-mediated exchange of ideas among learners. Unfortunately, in too many classrooms, academic discourse is stifled by the teacher's own practices. In one well-known study about the lack of discourse, students experienced an average of 50 seconds of open exchange of ideas in 8th grade English classrooms and an even more dismal 15 seconds in 9th grade, leading the researchers to label this as "monologic instruction" (Nystrand & Gamoran, 1991).

Telling isn't teaching, and students must be actively engaged in the academic discourse of the classroom if they are to understand the content. Because learning isn't a passive experience but one that is innately social, effective classrooms require that a "sea" of conversation occur throughout the day. Students simply cannot learn through listening alone; they need lots of opportunities to try new knowledge on for size if they are to take possession of the concepts and apply them to novel situations. However, their relative ability to do so is influenced by their command of four aspects of academic discourse: the functions, forms, registers, and vocabulary needed in the classroom.

## Function, Form, Register, and Vocabulary

The conditions of communication—a sender, a message, and a receiver—are factors in academic discourse, both expressively (the sender) and receptively (the receiver). The likelihood that a message will be clearly expressed and understood depends on each participant's ability to understand the function of the message (to inform, question, command), the comprehensibility of the structure of the message (form), the relative level of formality used (register), and the precision of the vocabulary employed. In reality, these don't always stand apart from one another. If a student says to his science teacher, "Gimme the thingee!" he has made errors across three of the four dimensions. First, he has chosen the wrong function by commanding his teacher to give him the item he needs. He has definitely chosen the wrong register, because his tone is inappropriate for a student speaking to a teacher. Finally, his inability to choose more precise vocabulary ("thingee") makes his message incomprehensible. In this case, he has used a grammatically correct, if simple, form. Let's examine each element—function, form, register, and vocabulary—in more detail.

### Language Function

Language serves multiple functions that a speaker uses to communicate and learn. The linguist M. A. K. Halliday (1975) described seven language functions used by young children as they acquire language:

- *Instrumental*—to express needs ("Want more milk")
- *Regulatory*—to tell others what to do ("Give me that")
- *Interactional*—to form relationships with others ("I love you")
- *Personal*—to express opinions and feelings and to assert identity ("I like pizza")
- *Imaginative*—to relate stories, jokes, and humor ("Knock, knock")

- *Heuristic*—to solve a problem ("How does that work?")
- *Representational*—to share facts and information ("Velociraptors are small, fast dinosaurs")

All of these language functions are used in the classroom, though the degree to which they are part of the academic discourse may vary. The personal, imaginative, heuristic, and representational functions are particularly critical to the academic expression of understanding. Students regularly use these four language functions to inquire and explain. Figure 2.1 contains examples of these types of statements at the primary, intermediate, and secondary levels.

| Figure 2.1 | Halliday's Functions of Language in Classroom Academic Discourse | | |
|---|---|---|---|
| Function | Primary | Intermediate | Secondary |
| *Personal* | "This book is my favorite." | "I thought the main character made a good choice to stick up for his best friend." | "I disagree. I don't think that Truman's decision to use the A-bomb has served as a deterrent to nuclear proliferation." |
| *Imaginative* | "In my story, the princesses decide that they can fight dragons, too." | "That event in the book reminded me of a time when I got lost in the mall and couldn't find my family." | "If I rewrote the ending of this story, I would have Romeo and Juliet run away together." |
| *Heuristic* | "How many more counting rods do I need to make 18?" | "If I connect this wire to the coil, I think the circuit will be complete and the bulb will light." | "I don't know what *amorphous* means, but I noticed the root is *morph*-, so it must have something to do with change." |
| *Representational* | "The stem is the part of the plant that carries the water." | "The exponent shows how a base number is multiplied by itself." | "There are four forms of infection transmission: airborne, blood borne, waterborne, and vector." |

## Language Form

If we look back at approaches to language teaching, we can classify them into two major categories: those that place a heavy emphasis on teaching grammar and those that assume students will learn standard grammatical structures simply through using the language. Certainly students must, at the very least, approximate standard morphology and syntax in order to be understood. And as the context of the communication becomes increasingly formal, accuracy becomes increasingly important. In addition to the basic rules of subject–verb agreement and word order, each of the language functions described here employs certain grammatical forms that facilitate understanding and accomplish the intended purpose. Some forms of language are more acceptable than others in different situations. For instance, "You give me yesterday's notes" can elicit a very different response from a teacher or a classmate than "I missed class yesterday. Can I borrow your notes?" Similarly, when reporting on a newspaper article about a threat to national security, "a person of interest" takes on a very different meaning from "an interested person." Hence, students need to use correct language form in order to make their message clear.

## Language Register

A student's ability to participate in the academic discourse of the classroom community is further affected by his or her skills in traversing language registers. These registers are ways of describing the relative formality of speech, and when the registers are violated, the effects are noticeable. Martin Joos (1967) has written extensively about the ways in which registers are used in and out of the classroom, including the following five:

- *Fixed or frozen.* These are the traditional recitations of language that do not change, and range from quotations to longer spoken texts such as the Pledge of Allegiance.
- *Formal.* This is uninterrupted speech and can include formal public speeches but also includes classroom presentations. The

formal register sounds much like spoken language that has been written in advance, and it is recognized by its complete sentences, grammatical accuracy, and a formality of structure.

- *Consultative.* Incorporating elements of both formal and casual speech, this is the register most commonly used in academic classroom discourse. It is two-way in nature yet retains some of the formal structures around content. The more general conversational tones of the casual register are used as well, especially through interjections of other participants.
- *Casual.* More general in its content, the casual register describes conversation among friends. There are more social markers ("How are you?") and more sharing of information.
- *Intimate.* This final register is reserved for the closest relationships, especially family and very close friends. The speech is private and presumes extensive shared knowledge.

Taken together, these language registers can be a minefield for some students, because there are so many ways to trip up. In particular, the consultative language register necessary for academic discourse asks quite a bit of students: they are expected to adopt a tone formal enough to correspond to the setting, yet also to use just enough casual speech to keep the exchange conversational and friendly. Consider the sophistication of this academic discourse in a kindergarten classroom after a reading of the book *Strega Nona*:

**Teacher:** Why do you think Big Anthony disobeyed Strega Nona, even after she told him not to touch the magic pot?

**Lisa:** He couldn't wait to try it himself.

**Julian:** He wasn't listening.

**Teacher:** What do you mean?

**Julian:** She told him not to touch it, but he wasn't paying attention.

**Teacher:** The two of you have different opinions. Talk to each other about your ideas.

**Lisa:** Big Anthony really wanted to make all that spaghetti like she [Strega Nona] did. He wanted to be magical like her.

**Julian:** He didn't mean to be bad. He just maybe wasn't listening like he should.

**Lisa:** No, he was listening. Look at his face [points to illustration]. He heard her, but he did it anyway.

**Teacher:** Could you both be right?

**Both:** [looking at one another] Yes.

This conversation could have been derailed at any time by a violation of registers. If either child had reverted to a casual register, perhaps with a bit of "uh huh/nuh uh" thrown in, the teacher would have chided both. Instead, when the teacher inserted herself back into the dialogue, the students immediately stopped talking and considered what she said. They knew that the register of the classroom demanded that they stop their conversation to answer the teacher. (Whether they truly thought the other had a plausible explanation is another matter, Dewey notwithstanding.)

## Academic Vocabulary

Choosing an appropriate rhetorical style and language register is for naught if the accompanying vocabulary does not accurately represent the content. The ability of a speaker to choose the right word over the almost-right word makes it likelier that the message will be understood. However, vocabulary instruction is typically conducted in an artificial and constricted manner by focusing on individual words at the expense of their role in the overall message. This approach to teaching vocabulary ultimately limits learning.

Several misconceptions about vocabulary instruction permeate classrooms. Perhaps the most common is the idea that vocabulary is bound to the word level, when in fact vocabulary necessarily exists within the larger context of the phrase and sentence. Therefore, knowledge of a word cannot be examined without considering how it is used in a larger context. Whereas *pajamas* can be defined as a label for clothing worn for sleeping, *the cat's pajamas* takes on another meaning as 1920s slang for something stylish. If stated by a character in an H. L. Mencken essay, it connotes a worldly air. The use of the same phrase in a novel set in the 1990s would represent a person who is hopelessly out-of-date. Likewise, it would be developmentally appropriate for a 4-year-old to say, "Where's my jammies?" whereas most would do a double take upon hearing a 40-year-old man say the same thing. Vocabulary doesn't exist in isolation—it has denotative and connotative meanings that reflect on the message and the speaker.

A second myth of vocabulary is that one either knows or does not know a word (Beck, McKeown, & Kucan, 2002). In truth, there are several dimensions to knowing a word, and our shared knowledge of a word is likely to be harmonious but not identical. For example, we all "know" some words that we would be hard-pressed to define. How often have you answered a query about a word by giving an example instead? There are words we are comfortable with using in writing but not in spoken language (*notwithstanding*, a word in this chapter, just doesn't get used much in oral language). The reverse is true as well—we might refer to our *kids* when speaking of them, but in writing we are more likely to call them *students* or *learners*. Finally, we know some words at the definitional level, and these are the vocabulary words that seem to be taught most often in school. We teach *rhombus* and *alimentary canal, onomatopoeia* and *Alexander the Great*. Sadly, many students fill out endless worksheets with definitional labels but rarely use these terms in the academic discourse of the classroom. This tendency limits their ability to know the words beyond the definitional level, as they have little opportunity to apply them in context.

A final common vocabulary myth is that students will learn a word simply by hearing the teacher use it. This idea isn't far removed from the "telling is teaching" myth, but it's one witnessed in classrooms every day. In dominating the sheer number of minutes devoted to talk, teachers also diminish the ways in which students might use, practice, and gain control of their nascent vocabulary.

Much of the vocabulary development in many classrooms amounts to little more than labeling. While the teacher uses the vocabulary in rich and varied ways, student responses are limited to furnishing the correct label for a concept or idea. Consider this example:

**Teacher:** There's an interesting kind of volcano that is recognizable because there are a lot of loose rocks from previous eruptions that build up over time into a steep vent. What kind of volcano am I describing?

**Joe:** A cinder cone?

The problem with this kind of vocabulary development is that Joe doesn't get a chance to take his label-level knowledge to another level by comparing it with other types of volcanoes, or to apply his categorical knowledge to examples of cinder cone volcanoes around the world. More often than not, it is the teacher, not the student, who will make these more sophisticated connections.

Although myths about vocabulary continue to persist, there is also a growing agreement on the conditions that best support acquisition. Blachowicz and Fisher (2000) described four principles of effective vocabulary instruction. Students should

- Be active in developing their understanding of words and ways to learn them.
- Personalize word learning.
- Be immersed in words.
- Build on multiple sources of information to learn words through repeated exposure. (p. 504)

The commonality among these instructional principles is that it places the student at the center of the learning. Vocabulary, then, is not something that is done *to* students but, rather, *with* them. Students' active participation and engagement are crucial to vocabulary acquisition, and the challenge in classrooms is to create an environment that allows them to use terms in speech and writing. Again, academic discourse becomes the ideal vehicle to learn new vocabulary.

Language functions, forms, registers, and vocabulary do not stand apart from academic discourse; they are elemental to the discourse.

In addition to these four components, variances in the academic language styles are associated with specific disciplines or content areas. In the next section, we will discuss these academic discourse patterns across the curriculum.

## Academic Discourse Across Content

Most educators acknowledge that mastery of a content area entails, in part, the ability to "talk the math" or "talk the science." Consider times when you have been at a large social gathering such as a wedding, filled with lots of people you don't know. How is it that you manage to find the other educators in the crowd? Was there something in their discourse that let you know they were classroom teachers, or administrators, or noninstructional employees? Perhaps you overheard the use of some terminology that suggested they were involved with schools, or they disclosed specific content knowledge that only an employee of the district would know. Maybe it was something as simple as one adult turning to another and stating, "You need to . . ."—real tip-off! Discourse patterns are subtle, but they are sure signs that a person can "talk the talk."

Just as types of discourse vary from one profession to another, so too do they vary among content areas. Students need to understand the different types of discourse needed across their schooling day. This is especially important for English language learners, who may not yet possess the flexibility of language that facilitates adaptation to the discourse styles of different content areas.

### Academic Discourse in English Language Arts

Given the content emphasis on literature, creative writing, and the like, it comes as no surprise that a common academic discourse pattern centers on narrative structures. This begins in the earliest grades, when children are asked to share personal anecdotes and, later, to make personal connections to what they have read (Kantor, Green, Bradley, & Lin, 1992). These academic discourses become more complicated as students enter middle school and are expected to clarify their understanding of a text and employ problem-solving techniques (heuristics) to support their comprehension when they lose meaning. Even more complex are the skills required to write expository text (e.g., organizing information for a research report). Classroom practices that provide opportunity for students to talk about what they are learning can scaffold both reading and writing. Reciprocal teaching for discussing text is ideal (Palincsar & Brown, 1986). This framework assigns roles to each of the four members of a peer-led discussion group: summarizer, questioner, clarifier, and predictor. As we will explore in greater detail in Chapter 4, students can use this instructional routine to incorporate academic language into their group discussions.

## Academic Discourse in Mathematics

Narrative structures are of less value in mathematics than they are in the English language arts classroom. Hicks (1995) points out that of the six standards developed by the National Council of Teachers of Mathematics, three involve discourse as it applies to the roles of the teacher and the students, as well as tools that support these conversations. She further describes the expectation that "students become young mathematicians, engaging in verbal conjecturing that is subject to public questioning" (p. 79). In fact, lesson study, a well-known approach to mathematics teaching developed in Japan, has been considered revolutionary because it causes teachers to shift their focus from presenting content to listening and observing how students are learning (Fernandez, Yoshida, & Stigler, 1992).

## Academic Discourse in Science

Although closely related to mathematics discourse, science is unique in its emphasis on inquiry as the basis for learning. The field of science education has been steadily moving away from the process-skills approach of the 1970s, which focused on learning the steps, toward

a curriculum that encourages students to construct their own problems and apply scientific reasoning to solve them (Palincsar, Anderson, & David, 1993). In particular, this means that students must
know how to ask questions, form hypotheses, interpret findings, and
collaborate with others in these pursuits. The Seeds of Science/Roots
of Reading project on scientific literacy at the University of California
at Berkeley describes four modes of inquiry necessary for academic
discourse:

- Searching for evidence
- Making inferences from the evidence to create an explanation
- Probing to find new evidence
- Changing explanations in the face of new evidence (Barber,
  2006, p. 2)

Clearly science places a high value not only on the use of the
technical vocabulary of the content but also on one's ability to
embed an explanation within an inquiry. Consider this exchange
among three students in a high school biology class as they attempt
to understand the findings of a lab experiment they initiated three
days earlier. The students had collected saliva samples from their
mouths and had grown them in agar dishes. Other dishes contained
samples swabbed from other areas of the school. They are now
examining the results:

**Jake:** Man, that's gross! Look at all this crud in my mouth! [points
to dish]

**Kelly:** I've got the same thing. There's stuff all over it.

**Jake:** Bacteria.

**Maria:** Exactly. Look, you can trace the swab marks.

**Kelly:** But compare it to the room samples we collected. There's way
less bacteria on the room sample collection plates.

**Jake:** So what does that say about the comparison?

**Kelly:** Well, our mouths are way more disgusting than our classroom.

**Maria:** Yeah, but is that really the conclusion? We have to write it up in the lab report.

**Jake:** Nah, it's more than that. We can say that based on our samples, there was more bacteria present in human mouths than on classroom surfaces.

**Kelly:** But we can't comment on whether the bacteria from our mouths or the classroom are harmful.

**Maria:** 'Cause we don't know that yet.

**Jake:** Well, that's what I want to know. There might be less bacteria on the classroom surfaces, but what if it's more harmful? How could we find that out?

**Kelly:** You know what Mr. Walsh [teacher] will want. We gotta write up a hypothesis.

**Jake:** Yeah, but it would be cool! Let's find out how we can test these samples for dangerous bacteria.

Notice that the academic discourse these students use contains very little of the narrative discourse used in language arts, focusing instead on drawing conclusions and analyzing for missing information. By the end of the experiment, the students have already shifted their thinking to acquisition of new information in order to answer their questions. In addition, they use technical vocabulary (*bacteria, hypothesis*) and the language of the science laboratory (*samples, harmful, surfaces*) in their discussion.

## Academic Discourse in History

The discourse style valued in history classrooms focuses on analysis and interpretation. Because history itself is not static but evolves through emergence of new sources of information and deepening understanding of the influence of events, history students must question sources, challenge assumptions, and consider various viewpoints.

Therefore, argumentation, persuasion, and analysis are necessary in classroom discourse.

Point-of-view analysis is an important tool to the historian, as it allows for critical interpretations of source material. Sam Wineburg (1991), the noted history educator, reported on the results of a comparative study of historians and 12th grade history students to determine the ways in which they approached materials differently. He found that the most significant difference was in checking the source of the information in order to consider the point of view of the author and thus determining the veracity of the information. Although the high school participants were all considered to be good students, their passive acceptance of the viewpoints presented in the documents suggested that they had not taken on the tools of analysis necessary for understanding history.

A common method for teaching point of view in the history classroom is through the use of debates, mock trials, and Socratic seminars. These arrangements all place a high demand on the academic discourse skills of the participants. Many teachers offer guidelines for successful participation in these exchanges and create rubrics for students to use to assess themselves. Guidelines are along the following lines:

- Listen as an ally.
- Make connections to the comments of others.
- Pass if you don't have something to offer at that moment.
- Use accurate information to support your claims.
- Accept the questions of others in the spirit of learning.

The discourse demands of these instructional activities press students' linguistic resources, both social and academic. To a far greater extent than other content discourses, students must draw upon interactional, personal, and representative functions of language while maintaining a collaborative language register. Students who possess strong content knowledge but lack the social language skills to participate positively will struggle with these activities.

Another necessary discourse of the history classroom is analysis and interpretation of bias. Closely related to point of view, this type of discourse also requires that students consider the source of information. Biased information in history can consist of obvious pieces of propaganda, but most is much more subtle. Therefore, inductive reasoning through questioning—that is, open-ended queries that are likely to initially go unanswered—is used to analyze information. The answers to questions emerge as more questions are asked. For example, students examining an artifact for bias need to be able to pose questions like these:

- Where did this artifact come from?
- What do we know about the person or organization that created this artifact?
- Did this artifact result in harm to an individual or group of people?
- Do we think that harm was intentional?
- What might have been the reaction of the person or group who was the subject of this?

## Academic Discourse Versus Social Discourse

Styles of discourse vary significantly from one discipline to another, but one thing that they do have in common is that they all require the use of academic language and vocabulary. This point is particularly important when we discuss instruction for English language learners. When students who are not native or proficient speakers of English first enroll in schools in the United States, they are typically placed in a class where they focus on learning survival language—that is, the language required to understand and express themselves in common situations. Students can acquire this social language fairly rapidly, communicating with peers and teachers about a variety of familiar topics. At this point in their language development, it is not uncommon for students to be expected to participate in the full range of classroom activities, with little regard for their continuing language needs. Yet the gap between the language they have thus far acquired and the language needed for discussing academic content remains wide. The knowledge and skills required to use academic language are of a much more complex nature than those needed for social language and academic language (Figure 2.2).

| Figure 2.2 | Difference Between Social and Academic English Proficiency | |
|---|---|---|
| Element | Social English | Academic English |
| Language domain | Listening and speaking are more common than reading and writing. | Reading and writing are required more than listening and speaking. |
| Accuracy | Repetitions, sentence fragments, and other minor errors are acceptable. | One hundred percent accuracy in grammar and precise use of vocabulary are expected. |
| Linguistic function | Common functions include describing, seeking information, and managing conversation. | Common functions require complex language structures (e.g., persuading, analyzing, interpreting, hypothesizing). |
| Cognitive demand | Conversation is generally highly contextualized around familiar topics. | Oral and written activities provide fewer contextual clues around less familiar topics. Prior knowledge of content and language is key. |
| Language structure | Simple present, past, and future verb tenses appear frequently in short, simple sentences. | Complex and passive verb tenses, participial phrases and auxiliaries, compound sentences, and the like are frequently used. |
| Vocabulary | Fewer and less complex words are most common. | A large number of words and word forms, often with specialized meanings, is required. |

*Source:* Adapted from R. Scarcella & R. Rumberger (2000), "Academic English Key to Long Term Success in School," *University of California Linguistic Minority Research Institute Newsletter, 9,* 4 (Santa Barbara, CA). Used with permission.

## Summary

As we consider the complexities of oral and written academic discourse in the classroom, we must consider how we can support students in bridging the gap between social and academic language. In the remaining chapters of this book, we will explore how student talk can provide that support and how to structure that talk in order to move students to a more profound ability to communicate their thinking about the entire range of complex academic topics they will encounter in their schooling and in their professional lives.

# Planning for
# Purposeful Talk

*Purposeful talk is one of the major means through which children construct and refine their understandings of language. Talk should underpin all language activities.*

—Education Department of
Western Australia (1996, p. 14)

Purposeful talk is also one of the main ways in which children develop their understandings of new concepts. As such, it becomes the kingpin around which instructional tasks revolve. It is integral to all components of a lesson—from teacher modeling and guiding to both collaborative and independent tasks. When we keep the importance of talk in mind, we can build units of study and daily lessons on a foundation of collaborative tasks that provide multiple opportunities for students to talk, question, discuss, clarify, and create new understandings through their interactions with others.

Although talk is a key ingredient in every lesson, it is not the purpose of a lesson but the means to an end: the development of a skill or understanding of a concept. We must therefore plan carefully and purposefully, using talk as a tool to build students' understanding. We must plan meaningful student interactions that occur within an authentic context, explicitly teach the language that students need to be able to engage in academic discourse about content, and always, always link their talk to reading and writing.

Regardless of the domain, we use language to communicate with others. When we talk (language domain) with our colleagues (audience), we don't simply practice verb conjugations; rather, we use a variety of verb tenses to recount the events of a faculty meeting (purpose). When we write (language domain) a letter of application to a prospective employer (audience), we don't write a list of words, all spelled correctly with definitions and example sentences; rather, we use a variety of words and grammatical structures to persuade them to hire us (purpose). Each of these interactions requires us to use language for an authentic purpose and an authentic audience. Yet, traditionally, English language learners have been asked to recite dialogues, complete grammar worksheets, and memorize vocabulary—activities they are unlikely to encounter in life. As we saw in the previous chapters, no matter the subject area, students spend little time talking in any part of their day. How, then, can we design lessons that ask students to engage in meaningful interaction with authentic purposes?

In this chapter, we reconsider instructional planning through the lens of academic oral discourse, especially as it applies to English language learners. As we consider each element of a lesson, we will include questions you can use to guide planning for talk. We don't wish to rehash basic elements of lesson planning but, rather, to link what is known about language development, instructional design, and students who are learning English while learning content in English.

## Planning for Academic Oral Discourse

### Using the Standards

As described in Chapter 1, proficiency in a language entails far more than simply being able to converse. It means listening, speaking, reading, and writing in a variety of situations for a variety of reasons.

Although proficiency in each of these domains may develop at different rates for different students, they are mutually supportive and best taught in an integrated manner. Oral language tasks do not end with the conversation but serve to scaffold learning, allowing students to activate their thinking before they read or to clarify their understanding and their use of language in preparation to write.

Planning for oral discourse begins like any other instructional planning—with students' needs and with the standards. Teachers of English to Speakers of Other Languages identifies five standards for developing proficiency in English (see Figure 3.1). The central tenet of all five standards is that we use language to communicate. The first standard addresses the purposes of that communication; the other four focus on using language to communicate information, ideas, and concepts within the core content areas—English language arts, mathematics, science, and social studies.

| Figure 3.1 | TESOL PreK–12 English Language Proficiency Standards |
| --- | --- |
| Standard 1 | English language learners **communicate** for **social**, **intercultural**, and **instructional** purposes within the school setting. |
| Standard 2 | English language learners **communicate** information, ideas, and concepts necessary for academic success in the area of **language arts**. |
| Standard 3 | English language learners **communicate** information, ideas, and concepts necessary for academic success in the area of **mathematics**. |
| Standard 4 | English language learners **communicate** information, ideas, and concepts necessary for academic success in the area of **science**. |
| Standard 5 | English language learners **communicate** information, ideas, and concepts necessary for academic success in the area of **social studies**. |

*Source:* TESOL (2006), *PreK–12 English Language Proficiency Standards: Augmentation of the World-Class Instructional Design and Assessment (WIDA) Consortium English Language Proficiency Standards* (Alexandria, VA: Author), p. 28. Used with permission.

The sample performance indicators in TESOL's English language proficiency (ELP) standards describe the expected performance level for each of five proficiency levels and offer ideas for scaffolding instruction so that students will reach that performance level. They do not reflect all of the content students must learn in all the disciplines, but they can be helpful as templates for planning instruction that integrates language and content. Each indicator consists of three elements: content, language function, and a support or strategy the teacher can use to help students learn that particular content or gain proficiency with the identified language function. For example, consider this science indicator for grade 4–5 students at the Expanding level of proficiency:

> *Discuss and give examples* of uses of *natural phenomena* from *collections of pictures.* (TESOL, 2006, p. 43)

The content—*natural phenomena*—gives an example of the standards-based concept or skill you want students to learn in a given subject area. The language function—*discuss and give examples*—defines how students will use language to demonstrate their understanding of the concept or skill. And the support or strategy—*collections of pictures*—gives examples of how the lesson provides support for learning the concept or skill.

Using the ELP standards side by side with grade-level content standards can help you scaffold and differentiate instruction for students at different proficiency levels. In grade 3 social studies, for example, your focus might be community, local government, and cultural heritage. TESOL's sample performance indicators in Figure 3.2 demonstrate what you might ask students to do at each of the five proficiency levels.

Sample performance indicators show the relationship between oral and written language. For example, preK–K students at the Developing level of proficiency might *orally* present a list of materials needed to conduct a scientific investigation and then *write* a list using drawings, letters, scribble writings, and words with invented spelling (TESOL, 2006).

| Figure 3.2 | Sample Performance Indicators, Standard 5, Grade Levels 1–3 | | | | | |
|---|---|---|---|---|---|---|
| Domain | Topic | Starting | Emerging | Developing | Expanding | Bridging |
| Speaking | Communities<br><br>Local governments<br><br>Cultural heritage | Identify landmarks or people from pictures or field trips | Describe national identities, customs, or traditions using visual support (e.g., flags) | Relate aspects of local or cultural histories to a partner using artifacts or other realia | Compare aspects of local or cultural histories using visual support (e.g., multicultural picture books) | Interview persons, summarize, and report historical or cultural information from local sources |

*Source:* TESOL (2006). *PreK–12 English Language Proficiency Standards: Augmentation of the World-Class Instructional Design and Assessment (WIDA) Consortium English Language Proficiency Standards* (Alexandria, VA: Author), p. 66. Used with permission.

## Questions for Planning Instruction

### Using the Standards

- What is the content standard students need at this point in their understanding of the content?
- What content builds upon students' current level of understanding?
- How will I make the objective clear to students?

## Clarifying Outcomes

Once standards-based content has been identified, it is necessary to determine what the outcomes will be. We often think of these as the products and tasks students will complete by the end of the lesson. As teachers, we use these products to evaluate progress. Not surprisingly, this is the aspect of the lesson students are most keenly interested in. Once again, both oral and written language skills are necessary for success, so planning should include arrangements for ensuring that students are adequately prepared. For instance, Ms. Lennox, a 10th grade health teacher, furnishes her English language learners with a glossary of key terminology to use in the development of their personal fitness plans. Terms such as *cardio fitness test, aerobic activity, anaerobic activity, fitness, long-term goals, monitor, self-assess,* and *evaluate* remind students of what they will need to include in their plan.

## Questions for Planning Instruction

### Clarifying Outcomes

- What work, task, or product do I want my students to complete by the end of this lesson?
- What oral and written language skills will students need to complete the task?

## Establishing a Clear Purpose

Using the standards and the results of formal and informal assessments of student needs, teachers can plan instruction that develops both content understanding and language proficiency. We begin by establishing a clear purpose that directs the path of both teaching and learning. All instructional activities within a unit of study or a daily lesson build upon one another and lead toward that purpose. When we set a clear purpose for a lesson and communicate it to our students, we inform them of what they will learn and guide them as they make decisions about what to listen or watch for (Marzano, 2007). A clear purpose lets the students know what they will be held accountable for and helps us as teachers maintain the focus of our instruction.

A challenge for all learners, and especially for those learning English, is that the talk of school is decontextualized and requires students to discuss events, objects, and people that are not present. As Justice (2006) notes, "Decontextualized discourse relies heavily on the language itself in the construction of meaning," and students must use highly conceptual vocabulary in order to make themselves understood in the classroom (p. 66).

In actuality, each instructional event has multiple purposes. Teachers of English language learners have at least two purposes for each lesson: developing content understanding and developing language proficiency. If teachers simply focus on content, language learning will only occur incidentally; if teachers focus only on language learning, content understanding may not develop (Hill & Flynn, 2006). The importance of establishing both content and language goals has been well documented in the professional literature (e.g., Brinton, Snow, & Wesche, 1989; Dong, 2004/2005). In addition, students must develop social skills to accomplish tasks cooperatively and must use social language in order to interact effectively. To address these needs, teachers often establish a social purpose for instruction as well.

Put yourself back in the classroom as a student. How often did you receive instruction on a complex topic, only to be told at the end that you had to apply it in some way? It's likely that you felt a bit frustrated and thought, "Why didn't you tell me that in the first place?" You may have listened to the information in a different way or perhaps made a few notes for reference. What was missing was a clear purpose. A clear purpose involves three conditions:

- A *content objective* that includes criteria for successful task completion
- A *language objective* that teaches and provides practice in the academic language needed for the task
- A *social objective* that defines the nature of the interaction

Of course, purpose must be established in a clear and coherent manner with students. Many teachers do this by taking the time to review the purpose before the lesson begins. For example, Mr. Bauer is teaching the 6th graders in his social studies class about ancient Jewish life as part of the unit on the Israelites. He is about to break the class into collaborative learning groups and begins by setting the purpose. "Let's talk about the purpose of this assignment," he says.

"I've posted the objectives on the board for you." The objectives read as follows:

1.  Your <u>content objectives</u> are to construct a map of the diaspora that occurred beginning around 500 BCE and to use your map to explain the event to me.

2.  Your <u>language objectives</u> are to correctly use the terms *diaspora, scattered, disperse,* and *exile* as you compare the movement of humans with seeds.

3.  Your <u>social objectives</u> are to make sure that every member of the group participates in the discussion and completion of the map, and to use accountable talk using a moderate level of voice.

Mr. Bauer continues, "You'll notice that each group has a packet of seeds and a map of the Mediterranean. Read the chart I've given you about where Jews settled outside Israel. Remember that the Greek word *diaspora* means 'a sowing of seeds.' As I visit each group, I'm going to ask each of you to explain this analogy, using the targeted vocabulary."

The purpose set in Mr. Bauer's class stems from his understanding of both the content focus and the linguistic requirements of that learning. To determine the content and language objectives of a lesson, think about the cognitive function you are asking students to perform—describe, compare, sequence, and so on. Then, consider the vocabulary and language structures that students will need to use in order to describe, compare, or sequence, as well as to talk, read, or write about the identified content. Figure 3.3 lists examples of the relationship between content and language objectives in different subjects.

After designing the content and language objectives, consider the social demands of the instructional task. What types of interactions will students engage in during the course of the activity? Social objectives are usually behavioral in nature; they concern the ways in which students communicate effectively with one another in order to complete the task. At times, grade levels may collectively identify social

| Figure 3.3 | Examples of Matching Content and Language Objectives | |
|---|---|---|

**Language Arts**

| Grade | Content Purpose | Language Purpose |
|---|---|---|
| 4 | Describe how a character changes in a story. | Use sensory detail to give readers a clear image of the character and the changes. |
| 8 | Write a persuasive composition. | Use transition words and devices to create a smooth connection between ideas. |

**Mathematics**

| Grade | Content Purpose | Language Purpose |
|---|---|---|
| 3 | Determine the reasonableness of a solution to a mathematical problem. | Use mathematical terms to explain why an answer is reasonable. |
| 9 | Solve an algebraic equation. | Use terms such as *If ... then* and the equivalent to write a situation to describe an algebraic equation. |

**Science**

| Grade | Content Purpose | Language Purpose |
|---|---|---|
| 2 | Identify the steps in the life cycle of a frog. | Use sequencing vocabulary to describe the life cycle of a frog. |
| 10 | Identify the steps in the process of protein synthesis. | Use sequencing vocabulary and scientific terminology such as *nucleus* and *cytoplasm* to describe the process of protein synthesis. |

**Social Studies**

| Grade | Content Purpose | Language Purpose |
|---|---|---|
| 5 | Identify the causes of the Revolutionary War. | Use academic vocabulary to explain the meaning of "taxation without representation." |
| 8 | Complete a time line demonstrating the sequence of events that led to the Civil War. | Use sequential language to discuss the events that led to the Civil War. |

objectives to emphasize in class. At other times, teachers may use social objectives to address concerns specific to individual children who may be domineering, timid, or less willing to do their share. Here are some issues that may be addressed through the use of social objectives:

- Gathering and putting away materials
- Taking turns speaking in small-group discussions
- Listening to others and incorporating their ideas into projects
- Making sure all members understand the solutions arrived at by the group
- Asking for and receiving help within the group
- Determining roles within the group and doing one's share

## Questions for Planning Instruction

### Establishing a Clear Purpose

- What vocabulary and language structures do students need to use in order to talk, read, and write about the content?
- What are the different language proficiency levels of my students?
- What social skills will students need to use?
- How will I make the objectives clear to students?

## Building Background

We don't want students to simply talk; we want them to engage in highly academic oral discourse, using the language and vocabulary of the discipline to talk about grade-level content. And just as we prepare students to read or to write, we must prepare them to talk. We can facilitate students' participation in academic language–related tasks by following a sequence that builds background in both content and language.

We can prepare students to participate in oral language tasks by building background knowledge first. When students have background knowledge about a topic, skill, or concept, they can follow discussions, participate in conversations, and construct meaning even if the language is unfamiliar. As they listen, they can compensate for gaps in understanding language by accessing their prior knowledge. Through direct instruction, video, visuals, hands-on experiences, and small-group or whole-class discussions as appropriate, English language learners can acquire foundational knowledge and understanding that scaffold their participation. (For example, Mr. Barber shows his biology students a computer-generated animation of cell division before providing technical instruction on this topic. He knows that having his students see this process helps them understand it. He also knows that seeing this process will help his students attach scientific labels to the concepts they are learning, thus improving their ability to express their new understanding.)

Engaging in discourse in a new language is a complicated process. First we hear a statement or question, then we think about the meaning of the individual words, perhaps translate them into our native language, digest the meaning of the statement, formulate a response, determine how to express that response in the new language, and, finally, produce the response. All of this takes time, so we must provide students with time to think and to talk with a partner before participating in whole-class discussions. As they think and talk, students listen to and practice language, rehearsing what they might say in a whole-group discussion. We can prepare students further by preteaching the vocabulary and language structures necessary to talk about the content. We can also provide sentence starters or linguistic frames (discussed further in Chapter 5) that help them formulate responses. (For example, Ms. Arquentte meets with a group of students to provide them with advance instruction on the word *reasonableness* and how this word will be used in their upcoming math lesson. In doing so, she provides her students with language practice and linguistic structures that they can use during classroom instruction. One of the sentence starters she introduces is "My answer is reasonable because....")

Questions for Planning Instruction

Building Background

- What background knowledge of the content do students possess?
- What background knowledge is missing or incomplete?
- How will I activate students' background knowledge?
- What do I need to teach in order to fill in students' background knowledge?
- What language forms or structures will students need for this lesson?
- How can I preteach these language forms or structures?

## Asking Robust Questions

Teacher questions can either stimulate or inhibit student talk. As we saw in Chapter 1, questions that have right/wrong or yes/no answers do not lend themselves to discussion. We often see notes in teacher lesson plans that read "Discuss _____" with a brief note on the topic. But how will this discussion be structured? Will the teacher simply lecture the students? What questions will the teacher ask? How will the teacher ensure that a true discussion takes place and not simply a question/answer period? Thoughtful planning of key questions to ask during a lesson can ensure that the discussion is elevated to the level of meaningful academic discourse.

Questions that require students to use higher-order thinking skills lead to academic oral discourse. Bloom's (1956) taxonomy provides a guide to assure that we ask students questions at all levels of cognitive processing (see Figure 3.4). Creating questions that engage

| Figure 3.4 | Levels of Questions | |
|---|---|---|
| Level of Question | Definition | Key Words |
| Knowledge | Recalling facts, definitions | *Define, describe, label, list* |
| Comprehension | Understanding meaning | *Paraphrase, predict, explain* |
| Application | Using a concept in a new situation | *Construct, classify, demonstrate* |
| Analysis | Separating a concept into components; distinguishing between act and inference | *Compare, contrast, distinguish* |
| Synthesis | Using components to create a new whole with new meaning | *Create, design, rewrite* |
| Evaluation | Making judgments about value | *Critique, defend, justify* |

critical thinking skills and encourage students to talk requires critical thinking itself; it is not easily accomplished on the spur of the moment in the middle of the lesson. Thus, as we plan our instruction, it behooves us to consider the questions we will ask at specific points in a lesson.

Ms. Jackson, an 8th grade algebra teacher, develops a set of questions for each lesson she teaches using Bloom's taxonomy as a guideline. As she plans a lesson introducing the Pythagorean theorem, she lists the following questions in her notes:

- *Knowledge*: What is the mathematical formula that describes the theorem? ($a^2 + b^2 = c^2$)
- *Comprehension*: What does this formula solve?
- *Application*: Can you describe a real-life situation in which the Pythagorean theorem is used?
- *Analysis*: Why do you think $a + b = c$ can't work?

- *Synthesis*: How does the Pythagorean theorem relate to what you have already learned about finding distance using a coordinate plane?
- *Evaluation*: What mathematic principles do you use to map the shortest route for a car trip? Why do you think this is the best way?

Ms. Jackson explains that she uses these questions as a framework for planning her lessons: "I find that by developing these questions for myself, it shapes the way the lesson comes together. If I want students to be able to answer a question, I have to think about how they're going to know the answer in the first place." She often posts these questions on the board to remind herself of them. Other teachers use self-sticking notes affixed to the pages of the textbook.

## Questions for Planning Instruction

### Asking Robust Questions

- What knowledge-level questions willl ask during this lesson?
- What comprehension-level questions will I ask during this lesson?
- What application-level questions will I ask during this lesson?
- What analysis-level questions will I ask during this lesson?
- What synthesis-level questions will I ask during this lesson?
- What evaluation-level questions will I ask during this lesson?

## Delivering Instruction

Lessons can be delivered in many different ways. The best way is whichever one works for you, but asking yourself some questions can help you plan lessons that encourage academic discourse. Along with the basics—knowing student needs, using the standards, and assessing progress—a lesson that promotes and facilitates oral discourse also has the following identifiable elements: an introduction that stimulates thoughtful conversation, modeling and guidance to prepare students to work collaboratively, and time to synthesize learning through independent work and reflection.

The introduction, sometimes called the *anticipatory set*, should motivate and interest students and cause them to consider what they know (and do not yet know) about the subject. Ms. Kahana designed an anticipatory set to gain her 3rd grade students' attention using visual images and a thought-provoking question. When introducing a lesson on Native Americans of the Plains, she displayed photographs of landscapes from this area of the country, especially grasslands, prairies, and rolling hills. She showed her students a painting of an enormous herd of bison, as well as a series of images showing the harsh winter landscapes of the region. She then asked, "How would you survive in this land? Where would you live, and how would you eat?" The students immediately started speculating on the possibilities. In this way, Ms. Kahana set her students up for a deeper understanding of the ways of life of the Lakota, Apache, Osage, and Pawnee people.

## Questions for Planning Instruction

### Delivering Instruction: Introducing the Lesson

- How will I introduce the lesson?
- What questions will activate students' thinking about the topic, strategy, or skill?
- How will I capture students' interest?

As noted in earlier chapters, academic discourse begins with the oral and written language students hear and use in the course of learning. Effective teachers model the concepts they are teaching by using the strategies they want students to use, rather than relying on the "telling is teaching" myth that fails so many learners.

## Questions for Planning Instruction

### Delivering Instruction: Teaching and Modeling

- What modeling will I do to clearly demonstrate the skill or strategy?
- What points do I want to make, and how will I make them?
- What questions will I ask to stimulate critical thinking?
- What vocabulary will I introduce, and how will I do that?

### Planning Meaningful Interactions

Whether an assignment involves solving a math problem, creating a poster, or sharing written comments with a partner, we often ask students to work together. Admirable though our intentions may be, students can actually complete these tasks without ever speaking a word to each other. Quiet students may simply solve the problem or write their description and hand it to their partner. One student might take the poster paper and pens and create the poster for the group. Effective teachers of English language learners carefully consider the ways in which students will interact with each other and with the content, leading to increased engagement at deeper levels during teacher-guided, collaborative, and independent learning tasks.

As described in Chapter 2, students need to use a variety of language functions to accomplish a purpose—instrumental to express

## Questions for Planning Instruction

### Delivering Instruction: Guiding Practice

- What will I ask students to do to demonstrate their understanding of the skill, strategy, or task before I release them to work collaboratively?
- What questions will I ask?
- Which students need additional guidance?

### Supporting Collaboration

- What task will I ask students to work on together?
- How will I organize the task?
- What talking, reading, and writing will students do?
- How will I group students? Why?
- What scaffolding do I need to provide?
- How can I differentiate for those who need different levels of support?
- How will I promote interaction?
- What language and vocabulary do I expect students to use?
- How will I facilitate students' use of academic language?
- How will I ensure that all students are engaged?
- How will I make expectations clear?

### Promoting Independence

- What will I ask students to do independently to practice and apply their skills and understanding?

needs, heuristic to solve a problem, and representational to share information. Within these broad categories of language functions, we can identify specific uses of language. In the course of a small-group discussion, students may express opinions (personal), sequence information (representational), persuade (regulatory or personal), or ask questions (instrumental or heuristic). Each language function uses specific language structures, often complex and in a more formal register than students use outside the classroom. Students expressing opinions, for example, might need to use superlative adjectives (*most interesting, better than*), conditional verbs (*should, might*), or expressions (*I thought ...* or *in my opinion ...*). English language learners will likely need focused, explicit instruction and practice with these structures to make them their own.

### Assessing Student Learning and Reflecting

Sound instruction always includes a plan for assessing what students have learned and giving them an opportunity to reflect on what they have learned. English language learners may need a particularly broad range of opportunities to demonstrate their understanding, because traditional measures may not accurately portray their knowledge. Therefore, an assessment plan might include a retelling, completion of a K-W-L chart, an individual discussion, a performance, or an essay. In addition, students benefit from the chance to reflect on what they have experienced.

Mr. Hubley routinely asks his 5th grade students to answer a question on an exit slip at the end of every day so that he can check their understanding of both content and language. Sometimes questions are very broad ("What's the best thing you learned today?"), but more often they are related to specific content. For example, after a science lesson on conductors and insulators of electricity, Mr. Hubley used the last five minutes of class for a short writing activity. He asked his students to explain why they were safe in a car during a lightning storm. While his students wrote, Mr. Hubley visited with the three who were still at the Emerging stage of English language development. Using illustrations and objects the students had seen during the lesson, Mr. Hubley allowed these three students to collectively construct their understanding and explain their learning. The students selected a piece of rubber from the pile of manipulatives labeled "insulators," a photograph of a lightning storm, and a die-cast car to explain that the rubber tires protected the passengers from electrocution.

> ## Questions for Planning Instruction
>
> ### Assessing Student Learning
> - How will students demonstrate their understanding?
> - How will I know who needs reteaching, and on what?
> - How will I know what each student needs next?
>
> ### Promoting Reflection
> - How will students reflect on their learning?

## The View from Three Classrooms

Careful planning of the ways in which students will interact with content, language, and one another results in powerful learning experiences. Academic discourse can flower in classrooms where students are used to working and talking together, but perhaps the most successful interactive tasks are those where there is a need to communicate in order to complete the task. When members of a group have information that others do not have, or when partners solicit an opinion from each other, they have a need to communicate. These activities, called *information gap* or *opinion gap* tasks, require students to talk in order to discover what their partners have learned, experienced, or think.

### Academic Discourse in Kindergarten Language Arts

Mr. Velez, a kindergarten teacher, uses the "busy bees" strategy to create an opinion gap for his young students. Students pair up to share what they liked best about their trip to the zoo. The previous day, students used a chart with three boxes on it to draw pictures of their field trip to the zoo. In each box they drew a picture to represent the beginning, middle, and end of their experience. After talking about their favorite part of the field trip with their partners today, they will add to their drawings and then write a sentence to describe what happened.

Mr. Velez stands at the door and greets each student as he or she enters the room. As he asks them how they are or what they read last night with their parents, Mr. Velez draws a happy face on the first finger of half the students—those who are English language learners and will benefit from partnering with more proficient or native speakers of English. He also includes Sonjay and Michaela in this group, who are native speakers but shy and reluctant to speak. The standard, purposes, and outcome Mr. Velez focuses on include the following:

**Standard:** Students deliver brief recitations and oral presentations about familiar experiences or interests, demonstrating command of the organizational and delivery standards.

**Content purpose:** To relate an experience in a logical sequence

**Language purpose:** To use past tense verbs to speak in complete sentences

**Social purpose:** To listen to the speaker and share opinions in a friendly manner

**Outcome:** Students will tell at least two people about the part of the field trip to the zoo that they liked best and tell why.

The instruction proceeds as follows:

**Anticipatory set.** With the students on the rug in the front of the classroom, Mr. Velez shows a short clip from *Jungle Book* (1967, Walt Disney Productions). He then asks the students to think about one thing they liked in the film clip and how they would tell a younger sibling about it. After giving them a minute to think, he has them turn to their partners and tell them one thing they liked. He cautions them to listen carefully, as he will be asking some of them to share with the class what their partner said. When the students finish their partner talk, Mr. Velez writes "*Jungle Book*" on the board, draws a circle around it, and creates a spider map of the things the students shared. He then tells them that they will be talking to their partners today about the story they are writing and that, as they talk, they will be using past tense verbs and complete sentences.

**Instruction and modeling.** Mr. Velez uses two of the examples from the spider map and shows students how to make a complete sentence. He highlights the verbs and explains that they are in the past tense because they tell about something that has already happened. He writes "I liked it best because …" on the board and completes the sentence for each example. He creates a T-chart with the verbs— on the right side is the present tense form of the verb; on the left is the past tense form.

**Guided practice.** Partners select additional examples from the spider map and create sentences. Mr. Velez listens in on the pairs and asks questions to elicit complete sentences and more detail. A few pairs share their sentences with the class, Mr. Velez writes them on the board, and together the class refines the sentences and practices saying them aloud. Students add more verbs to the chart and practice saying both the present and past tense forms.

**Collaborative task.** Students return to their desks to get the charts they created the previous day regarding their trip. Mr. Velez gives them a minute to look at their pictures and think about what their favorite part of the field trip was. They stand up, and he tells them they are going to do busy bees to find a partner. He explains that, on the signal, they will find partners, show them their picture, and tell them what their favorite part of the trip was and why. He reminds them to use complete sentences and past tense verbs. He then gives them the signal, an academic focus word that changes each week. This week the word is *evaporation* because that is what the class has been learning about in science. The students know that when they hear the word *evaporation*, that is their signal to either stop or start an assigned task. Mr. Velez says, "Evaporation," and the students buzz around the room like bees looking for a place to land. When he repeats the word, they stop and quickly find a partner—those with happy faces pairing up with those without. Each partner shares. Mr. Velez says "Evaporation" again, and the students buzz around the room once more. They repeat the process yet again so that each student has talked with three partners.

**Independent practice.** Returning to their seats, students refine their drawings and write a sentence that tells about their favorite part of the trip.

**Assessment.** As students draw and write, Mr. Velez circulates and talks with them about what they want to write. He reminds them to use the verb chart to help with the past tense, and he asks questions to elicit more detail in their sentences. He makes notes on his log about what additional instruction each student needs.

**Reflection.** Back on the rug, Mr. Velez reminds students of the objectives for the day and asks students to tell their partners what past tense verb they used in their sentence.

## Academic Discourse in 5th Grade Social Studies

One way to create an information gap is through a common collaborative task known as a "jigsaw." Notice how Ms. Schmidt plans a jigsaw for her 5th grade students as they learn about the early explorations of America. They have just completed a unit on Native Americans and are now moving into a study of the European explorers in order to understand the mutual effects of the contact between the two cultures. The standard, purposes, and outcome for this lesson included the following:

**Standard:** Students trace the routes of early explorers and describe the early explorations of America.

**Content purpose:** To explain the routes, obstacles, and accomplishments of the explorers; the reasons Europeans explored and colonized the world; and the effects of the exploration in each culture

**Language purpose:** To write and speak using past tense verbs and key vocabulary: *route, accomplishment, obstacle, compass, captain, chart, course, exploration,* and *indigenous*

**Social purpose:** To ask questions and clarify understanding of a reading in their expert group and to share information with one another

**Outcome:** Students will complete a chart highlighting the characteristics, goals, and accomplishments of the early explorers in preparation for a written and oral report comparing two European explorers.

The instruction proceeds as follows:

**Instruction and modeling.** Ms. Schmidt begins class by setting the stage with a story about the age of exploration, painting a picture for the students of the events of the time in Europe that led the authorities to launch explorations for new land. She pulls down the map of what Europeans thought the world looked like, identifying the European nations and the destinations in Asia. She asks partners to discuss what route they would take. As students discuss what appears to be the logical and shortest route, she pulls down a contemporary map and dispels this myth, stimulating their thinking about Christopher Columbus and the westerly route he wanted to take.

**Guided practice.** Ms. Schmidt asks students to look at the 15th-century map and compare it with a contemporary map. She hands out a variety of short pieces of text and asks students to scan for the information to complete the first row of the explorer chart handout. She asks them to do a think-write-pair-share to describe what kind of person Columbus was based on what they have learned.

**Collaborative task.** Ms. Schmidt divides the students into heterogeneous home groups of four. Each student is assigned a number from 1 to 4. Students assigned to the second group are English language learners at the Developing and Expanding levels of proficiency for whom she wants to provide additional support in the form of guided instruction, linguistic frames to facilitate discussion, and differentiated text, including a few texts in Spanish. Many of these students share a common primary language and will be able to discuss their ideas in Spanish before determining how to express the key ideas in English.

In their expert groups, students read from a variety of texts about their assigned explorer, take notes, discuss their findings, and then agree on important points to write on their chart. They then rehearse with a partner how they will present this information to their home group.

In home groups, students orally share their learning about their explorer, and each student completes the explorer chart. Upon completing the chart, the small groups discuss generalizations about the early exploration of America.

**Independent task.** Each student selects two explorers to compare and contrast. They select a task from a list of possibilities, including a dialogue between two explorers, a summary, a poem, a newspaper account, a report to the king and queen, and a legal argument before the court to defend the explorer's claims. Students use their charts to help them include information comparing the two explorers in their writing.

**Assessment.** Ms. Schmidt asks the students to return to their expert groups and form inside/outside circles. The students in the first and second groups form the inner circle of an inside/outside circle together, while the students in the third and fourth groups sit in the outer circle. Facing partners present their summaries to each other. When Ms. Schmidt rings a bell, outside circle students move one seat to the left and each presents his or her summary to a second student.

**Reflection.** The class reconvenes, and Ms. Schmidt leads a whole-class discussion on what they have learned about the early exploration of America. As they talk, she develops a class chart for them to summarize their learning (see Figure 3.5).

## Academic Discourse in 10th Grade Biology

Mr. Barber's biology students have been studying the environment, most recently learning about the various biomes and the plants and

**Figure 3.5    5th Grade Language Chart**

| Explorer | Sponsor | Dates | Characteristics | Goals | Obstacles | Accomplishments |
|---|---|---|---|---|---|---|
| Christopher Columbus | Ferdinand and Isabela of Spain | 1492 1493 1498 1502 | Creative thinker; persistent, courageous | Riches for the king and queen of Spain | North America, a mutinous crew | Found new land. Brought back things people had never seen.<br><br>Led to the beginning of modern-day maps. Introduced the horse to North America, the tomato to Europe, etc. |
| Francisco Vásquez de Coronado | | | | | | |
| Henry Hudson | | | | | | |
| Ferdinand Magellan | | | | | | |
| Jacques Cartier | | | | | | |

animals that live in each. The essential question they seek to answer in this unit is "How are we connected with our environment?" They are now about to move into a more in-depth study of the relationship among plants, animals, and organisms and their environments. You'll see in this lesson that the sequence of instruction is not always linear, from instruction to modeling to guided practice to collaborative work; rather, it moves fluidly between instruction and modeling and guided and collaborative practice and back again. During the course of this lesson, Mr. Barber's students will develop their understanding of the following standard, purposes, and outcome:

**Standard:** Students know that the stability of producers and decomposers is vital to an ecosystem.

**Content purpose:** To classify organisms

**Language purpose:** To use scientific terminology to explain how producers and decomposers affect the environment

**Social purpose:** To share opinions and ideas

**Outcome:** Students will write a paragraph explaining how producers and decomposers affect the environment.

The lesson proceeds as follows:

**Anticipatory set.** Mr. Barber reminds students of the essential question for this unit. He then asks them to complete an anticipation guide with several statements related to the topic of ecology (see Figure 3.6). They read the statements individually; decide whether they agree or disagree; and then discuss them with a partner, coming to consensus and writing a justification for each statement. They will return to this guide at the end of the unit to see whether any of their opinions or understandings have changed.

Mr. Barber knows his students have a great deal of background knowledge about ecology and the environment that he can activate and build upon. He has collected a variety of pictures related to the environment and posted them on chart paper around the room. In

| Figure 3.6 | Anticipation Guide for Ecology | | | |
|---|---|---|---|---|

| Pre | | | | Post | |
|---|---|---|---|---|---|
| A | D | Statement | Justification | A | D |
| | | Eating fish can be harmful to our health. | | | |
| | | Because of global warming, polar bears are beginning to drown. | | | |
| | | There are seas and lakes that are vanishing from our planet. | | | |
| | | We will run out of fossil fuels (oil and gasoline) within 45 years. | | | |
| | | A pound of salad contains more energy than a pound of steak. | | | |
| | | 2005 was the hottest year on record since scientists started collecting temperature data in 1860. | | | |
| | | The United States is the number one contributor of greenhouse gas pollution in the world, contributing more than South America, Africa, the Middle East, Australia, Japan, and Asia combined. | | | |

pairs, students move around to each of the observation charts, looking at the pictures and reading the captions, graphs, and short text. They discuss what they see and write their observations, questions, and opinions on each chart before moving on to the next one. The students in this classroom have different levels of knowledge about ecology and different levels of proficiency in English. All are able to participate, and all have something to say about the pictures. The English language learners have the opportunity not only to talk with partners in their primary language but also to read what others have written and use some of the language they see. They are not expected to write in complete sentences—bullets are acceptable—so the focus is on their conversation and their prior understanding. This activity serves several purposes. It stimulates the students' thinking and allows Mr. Barber to assess their prior knowledge; students can return to the charts as they learn new information throughout the unit; and at the end of the unit, students can use the charts to review and reflect.

**Instruction and modeling.** When students return to their seats, Mr. Barber tells them that their purpose today is to learn about classifying organisms in order to be able to explain the effect that different organisms have on the environment. He gives each table an envelope with word cards and tells them they are to do a concept sort, sorting the words in any way they deem appropriate. As he walks around the room, he asks the groups what their rationales were for sorting the words. The groups sorted the cards in a variety of ways: by the environment they live in; by predators and prey; by plants, bacteria, or ability to fly. After a few minutes, Mr. Barber returns to the front of the room and asks students to take out their journals to take notes. He begins his brief lecture on the classification of organisms by talking about consumers and producers, teaching the students the more precise terms of *autotrophs* and *heterotrophs*.

**Guided practice.** Mr. Barber then asks the students to return to their word cards and re-sort them by whether they represent autotrophs or heterotrophs. As he walks around the room, he assists students and asks questions, always using the key terms—*environment, autotroph,* and *heterotroph*.

**Instruction and modeling.** Returning to his interactive lecture, Mr. Barber focuses on heterotrophs, giving a brief explanation of the categories within that classification.

**Guided practice.** He asks students to sort the word cards once again, this time into the five categories of heterotrophs: herbivores, carnivores, omnivores, scavengers, and decomposers.

**Collaborative task.** Students have been working collaboratively throughout this lesson. Their teacher has spent no more than 10 minutes as a giver of information. After each short lecture, students have worked together to process and apply the information, all the while using the scientific terminology they must learn. Their task now is to select two of the categories of heterotrophs and write a collaborative dialogue between them discussing their effect on each other and the environment.

**Independent practice.** In their journals, students draw a graphic representation of the categories of organisms. Next to their drawing, they write a definition of each category, with examples of each.

**Assessment.** Mr. Barber was able to conduct an assessment of his students' prior knowledge as they completed the anticipation guide, discussed the observation charts, and sorted the word cards. As they continued each succeeding word sort, he was able to gauge their understanding of the classifications. And in his weekly perusal of their journals, he will check the understanding of each student.

**Reflection.** At the end of class, students return to their journals and write a brief reflection on what they know now about how we are connected to our environment.

## Developing Instructional Practice

Teacher reflection is equally as important as student reflection. Just as we must provide time for students to think about what they have learned, identify strategies they used for learning, and set goals for developing proficiency, we must set aside time to synthesize our own learning, analyze our successes, critique our practice, and set goals for professional growth. You can use the rubric in Figure 3.7 to reflect on your proficiency in planning lessons that stimulate and facilitate oral academic discourse for all students. The rubric can provoke discussion among colleagues or simply guide contemplation on specific aspects of classrooms that talk.

**Figure 3.7    Developing Practice: Classrooms That Talk Rubric**

| Effective Practice | 4 | 3 | 2 | 1 |
|---|---|---|---|---|
| Communicate purpose to students. | Content and language purposes are clearly stated and include student outcomes. | Stated purpose includes outcomes but focuses on either content or language goals only. | Stated purpose is general and lacks outcomes or expectations. | There is no stated purpose. |
| Plan tasks that are engaging. | Frequent or sustained active participation offers choice and demonstrates consideration of student strengths, learning styles, and interests. | Participation opportunities acknowledge student strengths, learning styles, or interests, but they are brief or infrequent. | Participation opportunities focus on compliance or rote responses that do not allow for varied student strengths, learning styles, or interests. | Student participation is minimal and passive. |
| Ask questions that stimulate discussion. | Questions require longer responses (sentences) that reflect a depth of cognition and are designed to elicit varied response. | A few complex questions require a deeper level of cognition, but many are literal level and result in short answers. | Questions elicit phrase-like responses rather than complete sentences and are literal level in nature. | Dichotomous responses (yes/no, true/false) are required to answer literal-level questions with single-word, single correct answers. |
| Facilitate use of academic language. | Multiple opportunities are provided for use of one or more language functions, and they begin with modeling of academic language use and a stated directive requiring use of academic vocabulary. | Students receive multiple opportunities to use one or more language functions, but either modeling of academic language use or a stated directive on use of academic vocabulary is missing. | There are some opportunities for using one or more language functions, but the need for use of academic language is not modeled or explicitly stated. | Students have no opportunity to apply personal, imaginative, heuristic, or representational functions of language using academic vocabulary. |

## Summary

Figure 3.8 includes a number of questions useful in planning lessons that incorporate talk. When teachers plan for talk and clearly establish the purpose and expectations, students use academic language and vocabulary in authentic ways. Unfortunately, talk is limited in some classrooms. To increase the likelihood that students are provided opportunities to talk, and thus think, we will now turn our attention from planning to creating an environment and managing talk.

| Figure 3.8 | Sample Questions for Planning Discussion-Based Lessons |
|---|---|

As you plan your lessons, ask yourself these questions to clarify each segment of the lesson.

**Topic**
- What topics are my students interested in that relate to the identified content standards?
- What will they find stimulating to talk about?

**Content Purpose**
- What is the content standard students need at this point in their understanding?
- What content builds upon students' current level of learning?
- How will I make the purpose clear?

**Language Purpose**
- What vocabulary and language structures do my students need to use in order to talk, read, and write about the content?
- What are the different language proficiency levels of my students?
- How will I make the purpose clear?

**Social Purpose**
- What behaviors do I need to correct or develop?
- What social skills do students need?
- How will I make the purpose clear?

**Outcome**
What work, task, or product do I want my students to complete by the end of this lesson?

| Figure 3.8 | Sample Questions for Planning Discussion-Based Lessons *(continued)* |
|---|---|

### Instruction

*Anticipatory Set*

- How will I introduce the lesson?
- What questions will activate their thinking about the topic, routine, or skill?
- How will I capture their interest?

*Instruction and Modeling*

- What modeling will I do to clearly demonstrate the skill or routine?
- What are points I want to make, and how will I do that?
- What questions will I ask that will stimulate critical thinking?
- What vocabulary will I introduce, and how will I do that?

*Guided Practice*

- What will I ask students to do to demonstrate their understanding of the skill, routine, or task before I release them to work collaboratively?
- What questions will I ask?
- Which students need additional guidance?

*Collaborative Task*

- What task will I ask students to work on together?
- What talking, reading, and writing will they do?
- How will I organize the task?
- How will I group students? Why?
- What scaffolding do I need to provide?
- What differentiation do I need to provide? For whom? How will I do that?
- How will I promote interaction?
- What language and vocabulary do I expect them to use?
- How will I facilitate their use of academic language?
- How will I assure that all students are engaged?
- How will I make the expectations clear?

*Independent Practice*

What will I ask students to do independently to practice and apply their skills and understanding?

### Assessment

- How will students demonstrate their understanding?
- How will I know who and what needs reteaching?
- How will I know what they need next?

### Reflection

How will students reflect on their learning?

# Creating an
# Environment for Talk

As Deci and Ryan (1985) have noted, behavior is often determined either by controls in oneself or by the environment. Most teachers already understand that the environment, at least in part, determines students' behavior. For example, when students perceive the environment as caring, they tend to respond in positive ways; similarly, if there are distractions in the environment such as interesting things inside their desks, students typically fail to pay attention. Creating an environment conducive for student talk is critical in ensuring that students really do talk.

Creating this environment requires an intentional focus on the structures that promote talk and the same purposeful planning that we bring to teaching the grade-level content our students must learn. When considering this process, teachers should

- Know whether the physical environment helps or hinders student-to-student interaction.
- Explicitly teach the social skills necessary for collaborative tasks among students.
- Have the same high expectations for student talk as they do for reading and writing.
- Create routines for talk that allow students to focus on making meaning of challenging content.

- Activate and develop students' metacognitive skills and learn to use the best strategy for supporting the task at hand.

The investment of time in creating this environment for talk will pay off in student learning throughout the year.

Let's start by observing how two teachers create an environment that promotes collaboration, learning, thinking, and talk.

## Creating the Physical Environment for Talk

The physical environment of the room plays an important role in supporting oral discourse, both through room arrangement and through the visual supports on the walls.

### Promoting Talk Through Flexible Seating

Mrs. Fericelli, a 3rd grade teacher, has a rug area in the front of her room to bring students together for whole-class reading or discussion where students can easily talk with partners. She seats her students at small rectangular tables that are pushed together to form groups of four. This is an arrangement we find in many elementary classrooms—children sitting in groupings of four or six around two or three tables that form a pod. Most high school classrooms, in contrast, seat their large numbers of larger students in rows of desk chairs. And middle schools tend to be just that—in the middle: some classrooms use tables, and some use desk chairs.

We recommend seating students in groups of four around tables that are small enough to facilitate small-group conversation without having to use an "outside voice" yet large enough to accommodate group projects and supplies. This physical arrangement supports effective teaching practice in a number of ways. First, placing students in groups of four lends itself to a variety of configurations. Students can work with a partner, and then two pairs can easily form a group of four. Students can pair with the person seated next to them or across from them. Purposeful seating allows the teacher to partner students in different ways (e.g., heterogeneously or homogeneously) for different reasons without having to ask them to physically move (see Chapter 5 for further discussion of considerations in grouping). Four also seems to be a good number to promote engagement for all students—enough voices to express different ideas and perspectives, but not so many as to be intimidating to a student who is not yet comfortable in English. Figure 4.1 contains a diagram of an elementary classroom designed for classroom talk.

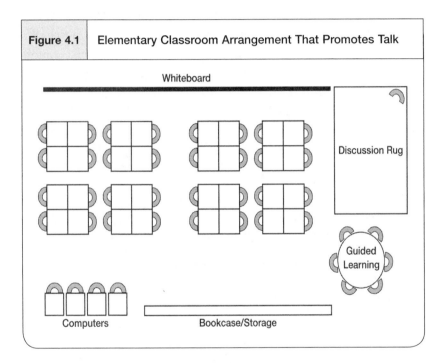

**Figure 4.1**   **Elementary Classroom Arrangement That Promotes Talk**

Obviously teachers must work with the furniture they currently have in their classrooms. Many schools are in the process of replacing desk chairs with tables and chairs, but funds are limited and change takes time. Still, teachers who are intent on promoting oral discourse still find ways to accomplish this goal. Ms. Sheldon's biology classroom is nearly filled with four rows of permanent lab stations jutting out from the sides of the room. She has no choice but to seat students in rows, four students to a row. So she has to be creative in her planning. Sometimes she has students in one row turn their chairs to face the students behind them, forming two groups of four with a lab station between them to serve as a table. Sometimes she asks students to move about the room, talking with their partners about observation charts posted in various locations on the walls or locating partners through a find-your-partner task. At other times, she has students move their chairs to the area in the front of the room for a fishbowl demonstration, choose one side of the room to stand on based on their stance on a controversial topic, or go to one of four corners of the room based on their choice of a topic or task. So, while we would love for all teachers to have table seating for groups of four, there are ways to create an environment for talk that circumvent the realities of a traditional classroom. Figure 4.2 provides a diagram of a secondary classroom in which student talk can be facilitated.

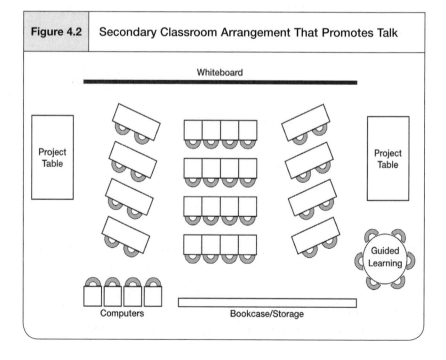

**Figure 4.2**    Secondary Classroom Arrangement That Promotes Talk

Whiteboard

Project Table

Project Table

Guided Learning

Computers

Bookcase/Storage

## Promoting Talk Through Visual Support

Visual supports in the room provide a valuable scaffold for students who are learning English. Here again we see the gamut, from classrooms with so many charts, pictures, rules, and samples of student work that items are dangling from the ceiling and the fluorescent lights, to classrooms with virtually nothing on the walls other than the fire escape plan and bell schedule. If we want students to use academic language in their discourse, it is helpful to post charts that contain that language.

The language of science can often seem like a foreign language for English language learners and native English speakers alike. Students need to be able to use words like *eukaryotic*, *Golgi apparatus*, or *alleles* to talk like scientists. Ms. Sheldon posts a word wall for each unit of study, adding words as she introduces them throughout the unit. Some words are used across units of study. These go onto a general word wall that stays up for the entire year. As students talk in their groups, we can see them turning to the word wall to look for a particular word.

Students do much of their reading in this biology class in reciprocal teaching groups (which we will discuss later in this chapter), stopping to question, clarify, and discuss as they read. English language learners who may have difficulty constructing sentences to express the sophistication of their thoughts can refer to the posters on the wall that list sentence starters for general discussion as well as for each of the components of reciprocal teaching: questioning, clarifying, summarizing and predicting.

Mrs. Fericelli's 3rd graders also use the walls of their room as a resource to support their discussion. They can refer to one of several word walls, depending on the subject they are discussing. Rather than an alphabetical word wall, Mrs. Fericelli maintains a separate word wall for each of the core subjects with the words categorized by topic, so if students are talking about geometry and measurement, they can look at the math word wall to find a word such as *perimeter*. As they talk with their partners, they can also refer to posters with sentence starters for discussion, question frames, or lists of strategies that they are learning to use.

In short, we can use the walls of the classroom to support more than the building itself; we can use them to support the learning that goes on inside.

> ## Creating the Physical Environment for Talk
>
> - Post visual supports that reflect current learning, key concepts, and vocabulary.
> - Cocreate charts that are clearly titled and easy to follow.
> - Arrange seating so that students face each other.
> - Use flexible seating arrangements.

## Creating the Social Environment for Talk

Classrooms where students talk are classrooms where students know each other and feel safe, supported, and part of a community. Getting-acquainted activities may be entirely unrelated to the content, simply done to ensure that students know and care about their classmates, thus creating an environment of trust. Of course, these activities can also be integrated with the content in ways that encourage students to learn how their classmates feel about a topic.

At first glance, it may seem that we don't have the time to spend on team building when we feel such a sense of urgency to improve achievement and prepare students for the rigors of higher education and the demands of the world beyond the classroom. However, building a sense of community results in greater (rather than less) productivity, leading to higher (rather than lower) academic achievement. The apparent paradox of spending more time off task in order to create more time on task is easily justified when we realize that team building creates an atmosphere of cooperation, collaboration, and enthusiasm for learning (Kagan, 1992).

Creating a climate of collaboration is particularly important for students who are learning English because they must feel safe enough to risk expressing their ideas in a language in which they are not yet proficient. It is virtually impossible to express oneself in a new language without making mistakes and being exposed to ridicule.

Creating a climate of collaboration really is not a matter of choice or style but simply one component of effective pedagogy. It seems the population of our schools grows more diverse with each school year. Classrooms are filled with students from all around the world, from different cultures, language backgrounds, and socioeconomic levels. The world of work for which we are ultimately preparing our students is equally diverse. Learning to work with others is as necessary for success as the academic knowledge of each content area. For students to gain the social skills to work with others in an academic environment, we must provide opportunities to practice those skills within an inclusive climate based on the belief that everyone has something of value to contribute and which celebrates cultural differences.

## Strategies for Building Community

As students enter Ms. Sheldon's 10th grade biology classroom on the first day of school, she stands by the door to greet them, hands them an activity sheet entitled "Find Someone Who ..." (Figure 4.3), and tells them to find a seat. The bell rings, and she introduces herself, telling the students that today they will focus on class goals and expectations as well as getting to know each other.

She explains that in this class they will work together much of the time, so they will begin by getting to know more about their classmates. She tells them the purpose of their lesson today is to introduce themselves and learn something about their classmates as well as to think about how science connects to their own lives. She directs them to look at the "Find Someone Who ..." sheet and tells them that their task is to find someone about whom one of the statements is true, asking that classmate to explain why or how it is true. Then

| Figure 4.3 | Find Someone Who ... | | |
|---|---|---|---|
| **What** | | **Who** | **How** |
| recycles their trash at home. | | | |
| exercises regularly. | | | |
| knows what global warming is and can explain what they think about it. | | | |
| has read anything related to a scientific topic that they thought was interesting. | | | |
| likes science because .... | | | |
| doesn't like science because .... | | | |

they are to write the student's answer and name in the blanks. To make certain that students are clear about their task, Ms. Sheldon models for them with a sample sentence, using a topic with which most students will be familiar. On the board she has written "Find someone who has lived abroad." She reads the sentence aloud and restates it to be sure students understand the word *abroad*: "Find someone who has lived in another country." She then asks whether this statement is true for anyone in the room. When Carlos raises his hand, Ms. Sheldon walks over to him, introduces herself, asks Carlos his name, and then asks him where he lived, when he lived there, and how long he has lived in the United States. She points out to the students that she is doing more than just asking Carlos to say yes or no; she is getting him to talk about himself and to give details about what makes this statement true for him. She explains that one of the requirements of science is collecting data and paying attention to details and that they will be asked to do this throughout the year. She then reads each of the six statements on the activity sheet in case there are English language learners who don't know all the words, and she directs students to stand up and find a different person to respond to each statement. As students meet and talk with their classmates, Ms. Sheldon moves from pair to pair, guiding and assisting as needed. Doing so also allows her to informally assess her students' prior knowledge and use of language.

Mrs. Fericelli's 3rd grade students work together daily, so she wants to be sure that all students feel that they are important and valued members of their team and their class. Some of her students know each other from last year, and some don't. So she begins her year with a personal interview. On the board, she has written the purpose of the lesson:

- Learn about your classmates.
- Ask questions to find out information.
- Make a brief oral presentation describing your partner.

As she tells the students what they are going to do, she also tells them why. She says, "In our wonderful classroom, you will be working with your classmates in pairs, in small groups, and as a member of the whole class. It's amazing to learn from others. To do so, we first have to learn to work effectively as a team. We must also show respect to one another and value the contributions of each member of this classroom." The interview tool provides her students an opportunity to learn about their classmates, make connections, and practice both informal and formal English.

She begins by explaining that good interviewers ask questions that encourage the other person to say more than yes or no and to speak in more than one-word answers. She refers to a chart where she has written "What sports do you like?" She reads the question aloud and answers it for herself, saying, "Baseball." She explains that, as an interviewer, she would want to learn more about this response and might ask questions about what position the person plays, what team or players he or she likes, and so forth.

To model the interview, Mrs. Fericelli asks Marco to come to the front of the class and help her demonstrate. Each student has a handout with interview questions and room to take notes (see Figure 4.4). She asks students to look at the first question and listen as she interviews Marco. As she asks Marco questions from the handout, she asks students to notice how she looks directly at Marco, nods her head to show interest, asks additional questions that are not on the handout, and makes notes of his answers to help her plan what she will say later to introduce him to the class. After asking a few questions, she asks students to form a line in order of their birthdays and then wrap around so that each student is paired and facing another student. She uses this strategy as a way to partner students randomly

| Figure 4.4 | Personal Interview |
| --- | --- |

Interviewer _____ Interviewee _____

Where were you born? _____

How long have you lived here? _____

How many brothers and sisters
do you have? _____

What do you like to do when
you are not in school? _____

What is one of your favorite books? _____

What do you like about it? _____

What subject are you best at
in school? _____

What is a career (job) you would
like to find out more about?_____

Why? _____

Who is a person you admire
(respect)? _____

Why? _____

for the interview because she wants them to all get to know one another and be able to work with any student at any time. Some of her English language learners end up with a partner who speaks their same language, and, as they conduct their interviews, they fall quite naturally into speaking that language. Mrs. Fericelli is not concerned, because the purpose of this task is to get to know and become comfortable with one another, and what better way to do that than in the language that is most comfortable for you? She does, however, insist that they read the questions aloud in English and reminds them that they must introduce their partner in English.

## Creating the Social Environment for Talk

- Model and expect respect for self and others.
- Teach and model respect for diversity of language, culture, and individuals.
- Celebrate accomplishment.
- Encourage students to support each other.
- Get to know students on both academic and personal levels.
- Dedicate time to building a climate of respect and collaboration.

## Creating the Expectations for Talk

For students to talk like mathematicians, scientists, or historians, using the language of the discipline, they must have multiple exposures to that type of language. Through teacher modeling of academic language, we can teach students about the register and the discourse style of each discipline, along with the vocabulary we expect them to use. This point seems simple, but without conscious awareness and intention, it can easily be forgotten. Modeling academic language also reflects the level of expectation we hold for our students. The best intentions of teachers can sometimes lead us to using "kid-friendly" language to the exclusion of the academic language that we want them to use. It is easy to underestimate the level of language that primary-age students can use and understand. We must be very intentional about the language we use with students who are new to English. Although it is important to avoid complex language structures in our explanations and discussions, students benefit from amplification of language rather than simplification. Restatement and explanation provide redundancy and allow students to hear the same idea in multiple ways, giving them time to process and interpret what they are hearing. They must hear and use new vocabulary multiple times before they can use it themselves.

Mrs. Fericelli wants her students to use superlatives like *most important*, but she also expects them to know and use the word *prioritize*, so she teaches the word and uses it repeatedly throughout the day. At different times of the day, she says the following:

- "We don't have time to finish everything before recess, so let's *prioritize* what we have left to do."
- "You've chosen three books you want to read, so you're going to have to *prioritize* them to decide which one you'll read first."
- "There are so many things to do at recess today—let's each *prioritize* our choice of activity."

As she looks at her vocabulary words each week, Mrs. Fericelli actually writes down ways that she can use them in a variety of situations.

Like Mrs. Fericelli, Ms. Sheldon knows that her content is full of new vocabulary that students must learn. She knows that her students will need to hear these words repeatedly in order to be able to read, talk, and write about the concepts. It is sometimes tempting for her to talk about the thing that carries *stuff* from the endoplasmic reticulum to the Golgi apparatus. It's easy, and she's used to talking that way. She knows, though, that scientists must use precise language, so, instead, she calls the thing *the vesicle* and the stuff *protein*.

She knows not only that she is providing additional exposure to a key vocabulary word but that she is also modeling the type of language that scientists use.

## Creating the Expectations for Talk

- Model academic language.
- Teach vocabulary and language structures.
- Provide multiple exposures to academic vocabulary.
- Expect students to use academic language.

## Creating the Routines for Talk

Sometimes poor performance can be due to a lack of understanding of the directions rather than of the content itself. Establishing and teaching the routines of talk is especially helpful for English language learners who may have difficulty understanding the language of the content as well as the language of the procedures. Teaching students the routines of the collaborative tasks allows them to focus on the content.

The steps in teaching routines for talk are basically the same as the steps for teaching content: teacher modeling, guided practice, collaboration, and reflection. (We leave out the independent practice step here because our focus is on the structure of collaboration. Independent practice would still be part of any content you are teaching.) When a strategy is new to students, it is helpful to begin with familiar or easy content. Posters that list the steps of the process can serve to remind students of what they are supposed to do. As they learn the strategy, they can apply it to grade-level content.

Listen in as students read and talk about grade-level content in a 10th grade biology class:

**Angel:** I just wanted to clarify that their goal here is to compare if the horses, I believe it was from China—

**Carmen and Clarence:** Mongolia.

**Angel:** Mongolia. I think they were trying to see if they were the same ones from back then as now.

**Carmen:** I have a question. So there's somebody that came from the Hebrew University in Jerusalem, right?

**Clarence:** They brought the knowledge of how to extract ancient DNA 'cause they have a sample of the teeth. I believe—and they wanted to do the process the right way.

**Trina:** I'll read the next section. I think it's going to be more about the process which they used it, and which they—analyzed the DNA.

**Angel:** Can I make a prediction? I predict it's gonna talk about the results and if they were reliable or not.

**Carmen:** What's a subspecies?

**Angel:** Subspecies? Uh, that's a good one. Probably a species that is pretty much related to it, or it can be like, very similar, or that was— that evolved.

**Clarence:** Probably took its spot or something like that.

**Carmen:** Oh, OK.

**Trina:** Uh um, what do you think they're going to get out of this? 'Cause they're taking it from the museum in St. Petersburg. What do you think is gonna happen?

**Carmen:** Isn't it gonna be old?

**Trina:** That's what I'm saying. Like do you think there's gonna be any DNA left on that? Or do you think it's so old, people been touching it maybe—you know, dust and all other stuff. I don't know—I just wonder.

**Carmen:** I don't think they're gonna have an actual result.

**Angel:** I think that they're gonna see a similarity between the sub ... species, the Przewalski old sample, and the new ones, and they'll be able to make a comparison between all three of them.

These students used reciprocal teaching to help them construct meaning from an article about ancient DNA. First developed by Anne Marie Palincsar and Ann Brown (1986) to foster reading comprehension for students with learning disabilities, reciprocal teaching has since proven to be effective for English language learners as well (Fung, Wilkinson, & Moore, 2003).

Before Carmen, Trina, Angel, and Clarence sat down to read the highly technical article they were discussing, their teacher had used easy-to-read text to show them how to do reciprocal teaching. This allowed her students to focus on the procedure without the challenge of the textbook, which is dense with unfamiliar ideas and loaded with new, technical vocabulary and complex sentence structure. Teaching a class how to do reciprocal teaching requires an investment of time. Palincsar and Brown (1986) recommend up to 20 experiences with aspects of reciprocal teaching before the full effects can be realized. Best practices suggest that students be introduced to each role individually, with several opportunities to refine the procedure before moving on to the next.

Ms. Sheldon teaches the instructional routine by first explaining that students are going to learn a process called reciprocal teaching that will help them to read difficult text. She points to the posters on the wall (see Figure 4.5) and tells them that there are four parts to reciprocal teaching—questioning, clarifying, summarizing, and predicting—and that she is going to show them how to do each step:

**Ms. Sheldon:** Starting with predicting, we've talked about making a hypothesis. Turn and remind your partner about hypotheses. Tell your partner what a hypothesis is.

**Hector:** [To Juan] Making an educated guess.

**Ms. Sheldon:** I heard Hector say that a hypothesis is making an educated guess. That's what a prediction is when we're doing reciprocal teaching. It's a guess about what the reading is going to be about.

| Figure 4.5 | Role Sheet for Reciprocal Teaching |
| --- | --- |

**Prediction**

We look and listen for clues that will tell us what may happen next or what we will learn from the text.

Good predictions are based on . . .

- what we already know
- what we understand from the text
- what pictures, charts, or graphs tell us

I think. . . . 

I predict. . . .

I bet. . . .

I wonder. . . .

**Question**

We test ourselves about what we just read by asking ourselves questions.

We see if we really understand and can identify what is important.

We ask different kinds of questions:

- Factual questions:
  Who, what, when, where?
- Interpretive questions:
  How, why?
- Beyond the text questions:
  I wonder if. . . .
  I'm curious about. . . .

**Clarify**

We clear up confusion and find the meaning of unfamiliar words, sentences, ideas, or concepts.

This is confusing to me. . . .

I need to reread, slow down, look at the graphs or illustrations, or break the word apart.

When I began reading this, I thought. . . .

Then, when I read this part, I realized. . . .

It didn't make sense until I. . . .

**Summarize**

We restate the main ideas, events, or points.

A good summary includes. . . .

- key people, items, or places
- key words and synonyms
- key ideas and concepts

The main point is. . . .

If I put the ideas together, I now understand that. . . .

The most important thing I read was. . . .

*Source:* D. Fisher & N. Frey (2008), *Improving Adolescent Literacy: Content Area Strategies at Work* (2nd ed.) (Upper Saddle River, NJ: Merrill/Prentice Hall), p. 25. Used with permission.

There are lots of clues on the text—bold print, charts, italicized print; sometimes there are even objectives listed for you. You might think, "Well, I'll just start with the reading." But all of those things give you clues to the meaning. And it's very important to examine those before you start the reading. So we're going to practice that part of it today: predicting.

After explaining each of the four components of reciprocal teaching, Ms. Sheldon hands out a short, easy text on how scientists are using geckos to learn more about glue. She places a copy on the document camera so students can follow along as she reads and thinks aloud, and they can see how she highlights the text. She has also given the students a guide sheet with each of the components listed in a box where they can take notes on what she does to question, clarify, summarize, and predict. There is also a place for them to write a reflection about how this process can help them read difficult text. Ms. Sheldon says, "I'm going read this text, and I'm going to let you know what's going on in my head as I read. Here's a heading, 'Putting Geckos to Use.' I see a picture on a wall, so I think this section is probably going to be about how we can use what we know about how geckos stick to a surface to make society better or maybe to make glues. I'm going to read and find out if I'm right." She continues with the lesson, modeling each of the four components by thinking aloud to make the process transparent. After modeling, she asks students to use their notes to share examples of when she predicted, clarified, questioned, and summarized.

So that the students can see reciprocal teaching in action, Ms. Sheldon asks four of them to read a new article in a fishbowl in front of the class. Again she uses a short, easy, engaging text, this time about cloning cats. And again she asks the other students to observe and write examples of each component. She stops them periodically to call attention to how they do each step. When they finish, she leads a discussion of the key points in reciprocal teaching. Finally, the students reflect on what they learned and how they think they can use this strategy.

Mrs. Fericelli also teaches her 3rd graders the routines of classroom discourse. Here, she teaches them how to do a three-step interview. She begins by explaining what the three-step interview is and what the three steps are, as follows:

1. Partner A interviews Partner B, while Partner C interviews Partner D

2. Partner B interviews Partner A, while Partner D interviews Partner C

3. Partners A and B tell Partners C and D what their partner said, and Partners C and D tell Partners A and B what theirs said

Because it is difficult to model a collaborative structure that requires a two-way conversation, Mrs. Fericelli selects Mika, whom she knows will be comfortable doing something new in front of the class. She tells the class that she will be Partner A and Mika will be Partner B. Mrs. Fericelli has placed a copy of a note-taking handout on the document camera so that she can model making notes during the interview. The topic she has chosen to model is familiar—pets—and there is a series of questions that are easy to answer: "What pets have you had?" "Which was your favorite, and why?" "What kind of pet would you like to have, and why?" As she interviews Mika, she makes notes on the handout, showing and telling the students that she doesn't write down every word but just some key words to help her remember. After Mika interviews Mrs. Fericelli, they turn to the class, and Mrs. Fericelli models how to tell the other half of their team of four what her partner says. She has listed some sentence frames on a chart (see Figure 4.6) and points these out to the class, noting that their language purpose today is to practice the language of giving reasons and that they should use these sentence frames to express themselves. She points out the verb tenses and key words, including *best*, *because*, and *someday*. Because she knows that referential pronouns are often difficult for English language learners, she explains what *this one* means.

| **Figure 4.6** | Sentence Frames |
| --- | --- |

I have had a _____ and a _____.

My favorite pet was my _____ because _____.

Someday I would like to have a _____ because _____.

_____'s favorite pet was her/his _____.

She/he liked this one the best because _____.

Someday she/he would like to have a _____ because _____.

Now it's the students' turn. The class has just returned from a field trip to the Museum of Natural History. On the bus on the way back, the students chattered noisily about their behind-the-scenes tour. Knowing they will have lots to say about the trip, Mrs. Fericelli has decided this will be a good topic for them to practice the three-step interview; at the same time, the activity will serve as a launch for a science unit on habitat. As the partners interview each other about what they learned about various animals and their habitats, Mrs. Fericelli moves from group to group, reminding them to use the sentence frames, helping them take notes, and guiding them in the process. To close the lesson, she asks the students to reflect briefly and talk with their partners about how this helped them remember what they learned on their field trip.

## Creating the Routines for Talk

- Teach collaborative routines.
- Identify steps in collaborative routines used in the classroom.
- Post charts of previously learned collaborative routines.

## Creating the Metacognitive Environment for Talk

Knowing *why* we engage in any academic endeavor helps us build schemas, focus on key ideas, and retain information. This is just as true of engaging in discourse as it is of being able to write a geometric proof or write a persuasive composition. When students understand the role that talk plays in learning, they can use it more effectively toward that end. Through explicit teaching and time for reflection, we can help students see how *talking* about the content facilitates *understanding* the content. At the same time, we can make the process of oral discourse transparent—especially important for those who come from a culture where rules for and beliefs about talk are different. Along with understanding the purpose for talk, we can encourage students to take responsibility for their behavior as well as their learning by allowing them to set the rules and take on a key role in creating an inclusive environment.

Mrs. Fericelli explains the purpose of the lesson and asks students to think and talk with a partner about why it is important to have rules for class discussions. She listens in as the pairs talk:

**Lila:** So everyone has a chance to talk.

**Anthony:** Yeah, you have to be polite.

**Aida:** And you have to talk about what you're supposed to talk about.

Mrs. Fericelli then tells the students that they will be deciding the rules for the class. She gives them three minutes to write down as many rules as they can think of. In their table groups, they share their ideas with one another using the "wrap around" routine. Students take turns reading one rule from their list. If the other students have that rule on their list, they check it off. If they don't have the rule on their list, they add it. Once each student has read one rule from the list, they repeat the process until all group members have read all their rules. By having each student read only one rule at a time rather than taking turns reading their entire list, Mrs. Fericelli is able to make sure that all students, including those at early levels of language proficiency, have an opportunity to share.

When each group has a complete list, Mrs. Fericelli asks them to share their ideas with the whole class in a "novel ideas only" format. Each student draws a line under the last rule on his or her list and stands up in table groups. One group begins by reading its list aloud; students in the group take turns reading so that all students are participating. Students in the other groups listen, checking off the rules they already have and adding any new ones to their list. When each group finishes, it sits down and listens to the others.

The students' next task is to come to consensus and prioritize their rules to determine the top 10. Mrs. Fericelli writes the word *prioritize* on the board, pronounces it, and has the students repeat the word as a whole group and then to their partners. After a brief explanation of what it means to prioritize and how to do so, Mrs. Fericelli models the process. She projects her list on the document camera and reads the first few aloud ("Listen when others are speaking," "Pay attention"). "Hmm," she says, "I think these are really important because if you don't listen to others, then you don't know what people are talking about and can't join in the discussion. But listening and paying attention are really the same thing, so we don't need both of them in our rules. If you're listening, you have to be paying attention, so I'm going to cross out 'Pay attention' and leave 'Listen when others are speaking.'"

As the groups talk about the rules, Mrs. Fericelli walks around the room, giving assistance as needed. Then, as each group shares its top 10 with the class, Mrs. Fericelli writes the rules on a chart, adding a star next to each one when it is repeated by another group. Finally, she leads the class in a discussion to identify the rules that will guide their class discussions. She will create a rubric for self-assessment from the list and will remind the students of these rules before they begin small- or whole-group discussions. Periodically, she will ask them to reflect on their participation in their groups.

## Creating the Metacognitive Environment for Talk

- Teach students how talk contributes to learning.
- Give students opportunity to create the rules for classroom talk.
- Encourage reflection on participation in group work.

## Summary

Creating an environment in which talk is valued is one of the necessary components for student learning. As students talk with partners about a concept, they extend and deepen their understanding. Structuring our classrooms in ways that promote oral academic discourse is one part of the equation; the *content* of the discourse is the other. As we discussed in Chapter 3, if we want students to talk, we must give them something to talk about. Students talk when we give them interesting topics to discuss and when we provide them with sufficient background knowledge to have something to say. Academic oral discourse permeates the classroom when we pique our students' curiosity, encourage them to question, and inspire them to investigate.

# Procedures for
# Classroom Talk

*The best way to get a good idea is to get lots of ideas.*
—Linus Pauling

It's a safe bet that the Nobel Prize–winning chemist and peace activist Linus Pauling didn't arrive at all of his good ideas by remaining silent. Chances are very good that there was a lot of talk going on at his Caltech lab as he and his colleagues worked out the problem of electronegativity and its relationship to ionic bonds between atoms. (Talk about academic discourse!) Of course, this didn't occur in an unruly or chaotic environment; the learning goals and social rules of conversations were just as important there as in any classroom.

As educators, we know that learning is social and that peer interactions help extend understanding. The idea that peers can scaffold new learning effectively for one another was one of Lev Vygotsky's great contributions to our field. Yet many teachers are reluctant to turn the class over to collaborative learning, for fear that they will lose control and thus lose valuable instructional time. We don't base this claim on observation alone. A study of the experiences of 1,000 elementary students across the United States found that they spent 91 percent of their days in either whole-group or independent seatwork, with only 4.8 percent engaged with peers in a learning activity (Pianta, Belsky, Houts, & Morrison, 2007). It isn't for lack of teacher knowledge, either, as 90 percent of the teachers held a credential, and 44 percent possessed a master's degree.

## Moving into English with Peers

As we have stated throughout this book, English language learners need lots of opportunities to apply their growing knowledge in order to learn English and learn *in* English. Their acquisition of academic language is certainly initiated through the modeling of teachers and reinforced and extended through classroom discourse. In addition, teachers provide more specific supports during small-group guided instruction. This approach does have its limits, however. For example, Zwiers's (2007) study of the practices of middle school teachers found that in too many cases the questions they posed to English language learners differed in complexity (concrete versus abstract) and the teachers accepted more superficial answers from these students than they did from native speakers in the same class.

Zwiers posited that students who speak English as a first language arrive in school with a higher "academic capital" that allows them to speak a school type of language that is valued (2007, p. 94). Therefore, they are more adept at using the discourse of comparing and contrasting, interpretation, evaluation, and description. But many English language learners, especially those at the secondary level, report that they have limited opportunities to interact with native speakers in their classes and that this is a factor in the separateness between the two student groups (Daoud & Quiocho, 2005).

Even in the very best of classrooms, the ones in which teachers ask sophisticated questions of English language learners and provide prompts to guide their students' thinking, learning is stunted without peer interactions. Marzano, Pickering, and Pollock's (2001) analysis of effective instructional strategies identifies cooperative learning with peers as one of nine research-based strategies with a large effect size (.78). In particular, small-group interactions with peers offer several benefits for English language learners:

- Repetition of key words and phrases;
- Functional, context-relevant speech;
- Rich feedback; and
- Reduced student anxiety. (Hill & Flynn, 2006, p. 56)

Although we believe a strong research base exists for creating opportunities for students to work together, we also recognize the reluctance many teachers have about using such an approach. Some have concerns about management—a fear of the proverbial cocktail party breaking out and an exhausting attempt to restore order—and some labor under the misconception that real learning can occur only under a teacher's direct instruction. In the following section, we will describe a set of principles for managing academic discourse among peers and specific strategies that foster learning English while learning in English.

## Managing Classroom Talk to Enhance Learning

The talk of the classroom is necessarily academic in nature and includes a variety of cognitive functions that help students explain their thinking and learn from others. For instance, students need to be able to compare and contrast ideas, ask questions, and describe phenomena. We find it useful to provide sentence starters related to the different types of thinking necessary in any learning environment. We post these sentence starters around the room and refer to them during guided instruction. In addition, we remind students of the language objectives for the types of language they will use in their collaborative learning activity. A copy of the poster we use in our classes appears in Figure 5.1.

When students are learning a new language, their receptive skills typically develop in advance of their productive skills. English language learners may indeed understand the discussion in a classroom, but they may have difficulty finding the language they need to express the depth and complexity of their thinking. Using sentence frames can relieve the linguistic load, allowing students to focus on

| Figure 5.1 | Language of Learning Poster | |
|---|---|---|
| Language objective | What is it? | What does it sound like? |
| To instruct | Giving directions | "The first step is…."<br>"Next…."<br>"The last part is…." |
| To inquire | Asking questions | Who? What? When? Where?<br>Why? How?<br>"What do you think?" |
| To test | Deciding if something makes sense | "I still have a question about…."<br>"What I learned is…." |
| To describe | Telling about something | Use descriptive words and details |
| To compare and contrast | Showing how two things are alike and different | "Here is something they both have in common…."<br>"These are different from each other because…." |
| To explain | Giving examples | "This is an example of…."<br>"This is important because…." |
| To analyze | Discussing the parts of a bigger idea | "The parts of this include …."<br>"We can make a diagram of this." |
| To hypothesize | Making a prediction based on what is known | "I can predict that…."<br>"I believe that _____ will happen because…."<br>"What might happen if …?" |
| To deduce | Drawing a conclusion or arriving at an answer | "The answer is _____ because…." |
| To evaluate | Judging something | "I agree with this because…."<br>"I disagree because…."<br>"I recommend that…."<br>"A better solution would be…."<br>"The factors that are most important are…." |

the content while they practice academic language. Some educators may argue that this framing of language results in shallow and contrived discourse, stifling critical thinking. And indeed, when students first begin to use these frames, their language will likely sound stilted and rehearsed. But then, isn't that the natural progression of learning any new skill? First we watch, then we mimic, and then we begin to appropriate, adjusting our use of the skill to suit our own style. Linguistic frames serve as a way to scaffold and differentiate both oral and written tasks for students at different levels of language proficiency. In this way we make the register, the style, and the word choice explicit, identifying the rhetorical moves that are appropriate to the purpose and the context and helping students make their meaning clear.

Linguistic frames can be used at any level—from beginning language learners to native speakers, from kindergartners to adolescents. Harvard University education professor and author Howard Gardner even asks postdoctoral fellowship applicants to use them to guide their responses: "Most scholars in the field believe _____" and "As a result of my study, _____" (Graff & Birkenstein, 2006). Examples of linguistic frames related to cause and effect can be found in Figure 5.2.

The academic language of the speaker is only one side of the equation—the listener also has responsibilities. Beyond basic social expectations regarding polite behavior, true discussion needs the active participation of others if there is to be an exchange of ideas. Lauren Resnick (1995) introduced the concept of accountable talk as a means of raising the level of academic discourse among students. Accountable talk governs the norms of academic discourse and requires that students ask for and furnish evidence to support their statements (Michaels, O'Conner, Hall, & Resnick, 2002). This ensures rigor and moves the conversation from task-oriented to concept-oriented learning.

In a classroom filled with accountable talk, students ask one another about their thinking and build on the responses of others. They cite evidence, ask for elaborations and clarifications, and extend understandings by using the statements they have heard from their classmates to form new ideas. We place a table card on each group's desk at the start of each collaborative learning activity to reinforce the need for holding oneself (and each other) accountable for rigorous discussion (see Figure 5.3).

**Figure 5.2    Cause and Effect Linguistic Frames**

| | Helpful Signal Words | Sample Sentence Frames |
|---|---|---|
| **Intermediate** | *if ... then*          *so*<br>*for this reason*    *because (of)*<br>*as a result (of)*    *therefore*<br>*when (cause),... (effect)*    *since*<br>*after (cause) ..., (effect)* | ▪ She was _____ because she didn't _____.<br>▪ If it _____, then we will _____.<br>▪ He believed _____ since _____.<br>▪ When _____ is added, _____ dissolves. |
| **Early Advanced** | *it follows*          *thus*<br>*due to*          *consequently*<br>*one reason for*    *hence*<br>*since _____, _____*    *the cause of* | ▪ It was discovered that _____. Consequently, _____.<br>▪ If _____ results in _____, it follows that _____.<br>▪ _____ has been caused by _____, thus _____. |
| **Advanced** | *even if ... would*    *accordingly*<br>*which in turn*    *due to the fact that*<br>*leads/led to*    *subsequently*<br>*leads me to believe that*<br>*once _____, _____* | ▪ Even if _____, we would need to _____.<br>▪ There have been _____, _____, and _____. This leads me to believe that _____.<br>▪ _____ has/have caused _____. Which, in turn, results/resulted in _____.<br>▪ Due to the fact that _____, it will most certainly _____. |

*Source:* Susana Dutro and Ellen Levy, *A Focused Approach to Constructing Meaning: Explicit Language for Content Instruction*, © E. L. Achieve/2007. Used with permission.

| Figure 5.3 | Accountable Talk Poster | |
| --- | --- | --- |
| **Remember to ...** | **Sounds like ...** | |
| Ask questions when you don't understand a topic. | Can you tell me more? <br> Would you say that again? <br> Can you give me another example so I can understand? | |
| Give a reason why your idea is a good one. | This reminds me of _____ because _____. <br> I believe this is true because _____. | |
| Ask for evidence when something sounds incorrect. | I'm not sure that's right. Can you tell me why you think it is true? <br> Can you show me a place in the book that illustrates that idea? | |
| Give evidence to support your statements. | Read a passage from the book that illustrates your idea. <br> Bring another information source to support your idea. | |
| Use ideas from others to add to your own. | I agree with _____ because _____. <br> _____'s idea reminds me of _____. | |

Students take quickly to accountable talk, and many appreciate the guidelines because they prevent conversations from going astray. For example, consider the following conversation in Ms. Hirano's 2nd grade class as four students discuss an ant diagram during science. They have been asked to talk about the ways that insects communicate and to decide what body parts are used by the ant:

**Kristina:** Well, I know they touch.

**Roberto:** But how do you know? You can't just say "you know." [*requesting evidence*]

**Kristina:** 'Cause I seen them wave their—their—what are those pointers on their heads?

**Ting:** Right here [points to diagram]. Antennae. [*offering evidence*]

**Kristina:** Yeah, antennae. They use their antennae to touch each other.

**Alejandra:** We're s'posed to use that word. Ms. Hirano wrote it on the board—*antennae*. They touch their antennae to see each other. [*using ideas from others*]

**Ting:** Do they have eyes on their antennae? Show me? [*requesting evidence*]

**Alejandra:** [examines diagram closely] I don't see eyes. [*giving evidence*]

**Roberto:** The eyes is here [points to label that reads "eyes"].

**Kristina:** Oh, yeah, that's right! They can see! They use their eyes to see. [*using ideas from others*]

**Ting:** Look how teeny they are. They must not see a lot of stuff.

This is a typical accountable talk interaction among young children and is all the more remarkable because it doesn't sound contrived. They still think and speak as 7-year-olds, but the difference is that they are listening to one another instead of speaking in parallel. In addition, the conversation hasn't wandered from the topic, because the students are accustomed to working together like this. Taken together, the language goals and accountable talk guide the academic discourse of the group, without imposing an artificial structure that limits students' thinking.

Of course, these four students didn't end up together through happenstance. Ms. Hirano created a heterogeneous group of students with varied content knowledge, language proficiency, and social styles. In the next section, we will discuss grouping considerations for managing talk in the classroom.

## Managing Talk Through Grouping

Although there may be a certain surface logic to grouping students homogeneously, the preponderance of the evidence shows that students of all abilities perform better in heterogeneous groups (Lou et al., 1996). It comes as no surprise that low-achieving students do worse in homogeneous groups because they collectively have fewer resources to draw from ($r = -.60$). There is a very small positive effect for high-achieving students when grouped homogeneously (.09), but average-achieving students benefit significantly (.51) from mixed-ability grouping (Lou et al., 1996).

The composition of the members plays a role in the relative success of a group. Bennett and Cass (1988) looked at the performance of groups where either the high-achieving students outnumbered the low-achieving ones or vice versa. They concluded that groups that were dominated by high-achieving students performed worse because the low-achieving student was left out of the process. This did not occur when high-achieving students were the minority in the group. A formula of two low-achieving students for every one high-achiever or two English language learners for every one proficient speaker may not be feasible for every classroom, but it is worth noting so as not to inadvertently set up groups that leave learners behind.

Achievement should not be the only factor taken into consideration when grouping students. Flexible grouping patterns that allow students to work with many classmates over time build relationships and broaden students' learning experiences. After all, the workplace is rarely a homogeneous environment—we are called upon daily to interact and work with people who possess a range of strengths and areas of need. Flexible grouping patterns are based on variables such as these:

- *Language proficiency level*: Students may be grouped together for a language lesson or heterogeneously to provide language models and facilitate sustained conversation.

- *Primary language*: Students work with others who speak the same language, allowing them to discuss new and complex topics in a familiar language.

- *Skills development*: Students are grouped together because they are working on the same skill.

- *Interest:* Students study a shared topic of interest or are spread among groups to serve as motivators.

- *Work habits*: Students are spread among groups to model work habits.

- *Prior knowledge of content*: Students are grouped to share topical knowledge.
- *Prior knowledge of strategies*: Students are organized to share strategic knowledge.
- *Task or activity*: Students are grouped together because the task or activity has been designed to meet their needs.
- *Social*: Students are spread among groups to serve as leaders or in other specialized roles.
- *Random*: Random grouping ensures that students come into contact with all members of the class and build community.
- *Student choice*: This pattern gives friends an opportunity to work together (Flood, Lapp, Flood, & Nagel, 1992).

To form effective groups, you must know your students well. When your classroom includes English language learners, you must be keenly aware of their proficiency levels in English as well as their understanding of the content of the task. Placing one student who is new to English in a group of proficient students may seem like a good idea, but in actuality, that student is likely to participate more with students whose level of proficiency in English is closer to his or her own: the English language learner will not feel as intimidated, and the other students may have more empathy and understanding of how the student feels. And, although it can be helpful to assign a buddy to a student who has just arrived with no English, be careful that the buddy does not do all the work and become a caretaker. Rotating buddies periodically relieves the burden of being the "teacher" and helps the new student get to know more members of the class.

Obviously, the ability to group and regroup students depending on the purpose of the task requires a physical arrangement of the room that facilitates movement. In Chapter 4, we saw how two different teachers organized their classrooms to allow for this flexibility. In some classrooms, the only solution to flexible grouping is to ask students to physically move their desks or chairs. At first glance, this activity may seem like an invitation to bedlam that takes valuable time away from instruction, but with a bit of guidance, students can learn to do this quickly and efficiently.

Students, especially those in elementary school, express a preference for working in mixed-ability groups (Elbaum, Schumm, & Vaughn, 1997). Students identified as gifted and talented in grades 5–11 acknowledged the social development benefits of working in heterogeneous groups (Adams-Byers, Whitseel, & Moon, 2004). When collaboration with peers becomes routine rather than anomalous, students settle into a pattern of work that is productive without being disruptive. Of course, managing noise and time also contributes to the smooth operation of the class.

## Managing the Noise and Time of Talk

We believe that mismanagement of noise and time poses the biggest barrier to teachers' use of collaborative learning and goes a long way toward explaining the dearth of partner and small-group work in classrooms. Although school administrators understand that a quiet classroom does not necessarily equate to a learning classroom, most of us worry that the hum of activity could devolve into the clamor of chaos and that our teaching reputations will be sullied in the process. This concern may be especially true for new teachers, who know they are under scrutiny and don't want anyone to think they have classroom management problems. Even the best-designed collaborative task can be diminished by poor procedures that fail to take noise and time into account.

### Managing Noise

Many children find it difficult to concentrate on the learning at hand when the din grows too loud. Much of the problem, we have discovered, is that students haven't had much experience at individually and jointly modulating noise levels, leaving it to the teacher. When working with young children, we sing the following verse from the campfire song "John Jacob Jingleheimer Schmidt," repeating it in a progressively softer voice until we are down to a whisper:

John Jacob Jingleheimer Schmidt
His name is my name, too.
Whenever we go out,
The people always shout,
There goes John Jacob Jingleheimer Schmidt
Tra la la la la la la

This activity is a great way to teach about volume and musical dynamics. We pair it with a visual representation of the volume using a noise meter (see Figure 5.4). There's nothing fancy about this aid—it is made using a large piece of corrugated cardboard, and the arrow is attached using a brad. We introduce the vocabulary terms *silent, quiet, moderate, elevated,* and *outdoor voice* and simulate those levels using the song. Older elementary students don't need the song, so instead we use a lamp with a dimmer switch—the lower the light, the quieter the class is expected to be. We practice being silent for 56 seconds, or working quietly for 24 seconds, or speaking moderately for 38 seconds, so that students gain tangible experience with understanding the relative levels of sound.

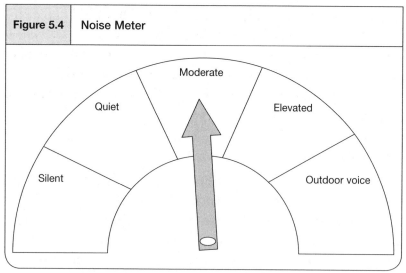

| Figure 5.4 | Noise Meter |
| --- | --- |

*Source:* N. Frey (2004), *The Effective Teacher's Guide: 50 Ways for Engaging Students in Learning* (San Diego, CA: Academic Professional Development). Used with permission.

We then tell our students that we will use these noise levels through our school year: silent when we are taking tests, quiet when working or reading independently, moderate—defined as loud enough to be heard by your partner but quiet enough not to interfere with another pair's conversation—when engaged in partner talk, and elevated only during small-group work. Of course, we never use an outdoor voice inside the classroom!

The noise meter is introduced on the first day of school and is revisited each time we move into independent work, collaborative learning, and guided instruction. Before long, the visual cue is no longer needed, and the verbal direction alone suffices. When the noise level does get too loud, we stop the class and redirect attention to the noise meter. We have seen other colleagues use variations of the noise meter, like a traffic light or a large "noise thermometer" with a red ribbon representing the mercury inside the tube. One of our secondary science colleagues begins the year by teaching students about the science of acoustics and the effects of noise on learning. The common denominator in all of these examples is drawing students' attention to sound levels in the classroom and giving them an active role in monitoring it.

## Managing Time

As we discussed in Chapter 3, releasing responsibility to students to talk with each other and construct their own meaning takes more time than simply telling them what we want them to know and asking a few questions of a few students to assess their understanding. It becomes particularly important, therefore, that we manage time effectively. By the time children are 8 years old, they show time-monitoring patterns that are similar to those of adults (Mäntylä, Carelli, & Forman, 2007). The rate at which they check clocks increases as time elapses, with fewer checks early on in a task. However, students aren't always as good at figuring out how much time is left. Setting a bell to ring at the end of an activity gets their attention, but it doesn't allow them to adjust their rate to meet the time requirements. A simple solution is to provide students with a means to monitor the time remaining. Countdown timers can be displayed using an overhead or a projector. In the absence of this kind of device, you can post descending numbers of variable intervals on the board and cross each off as the time elapses. For example, in a 15-minute assignment, post the numbers 13, 10, 7, 5, 3, 2, and 1 to reflect the increased clock checking that students will do. An added benefit of an overhead timer or chalkboard countdown is that it helps the teacher monitor time as well.

## Managing Linguistic and Cultural Diversity

Noise and time management aside, another challenge in using effective collaborative tasks is how to ensure that all students are actively engaged in learning. One common fear is that students will spend their time talking about topics that have nothing to do with the task at hand. There are also the issues of certain students dominating and doing all the work and of students who prefer to work independently. When we add in the elements of linguistic and cultural diversity, we add another dimension to the complexities of managing oral discourse in the classroom. Here again, purposeful and structured planning, along with teacher guidance and support, can maximize participation and learning for all students.

### Managing Linguistic Diversity

For obvious reasons, it can be particularly uncomfortable for teachers when students are talking together in a language that the teacher does not speak. Using the primary language in the classroom, whether it is the teacher speaking or students, is a somewhat controversial practice. On one side of the argument are those who believe that students must *use* English to *learn* English and that time not spent in English is valuable learning time lost. They argue that, for many students, class time is the only time they are speaking English, because they may go home to communities where there is no need to do so. We wholeheartedly agree that one of the primary goals for our students is proficiency in English, but one of our other primary goals is understanding of grade-level content, which includes progressively more and more difficult concepts as students move up the grade levels.

Consider for a moment this scenario. You are in a class as a learner, studying a subject you are unfamiliar with—perhaps stoichiometry, tessellations, or corpus linguistics. Would you prefer to discuss these new ideas in your native language or in a new language that you are learning—say, Russian, Portuguese, or Amharic? Language choice, like grouping, depends on the purpose. There may be times when students will learn more if they can talk about new and difficult concepts in familiar language. Of course, we want to be sure they are talking about the new concept and that they are on the right track. So how do we do this?

First, when we have created the type of environment we described in Chapter 4, where students understand the purpose of talk, are used to talking, and know that their ideas are important, we can trust that students will value the time to discuss and clarify their understanding. Will they do so 100 percent of the time? Perhaps not, though we would argue that the percent of time on task is not proportional to which language students are using.

Second, we can monitor student talk in a language other than English in the same way we monitor students speaking in English, by sitting with the group and asking questions, in English, to gauge their understanding. They must respond in English, which gives them the opportunity to use the language and vocabulary we expect them to use, with the added support of having first had an opportunity to clarify their thinking in a familiar language.

Finally, accountability is built into all collaborative tasks. Teachers may require students to complete a graphic organizer, write a summary, create a skit, or present their conclusions to the class.

Even when we require students to complete and turn in a written product as part of their collaborative work, this task does not necessarily translate into engagement for all students. Without careful organization, one or two students can end up doing all the work. In the last chapter, we talked about how to teach students to share responsibility, contributing to the discussion and encouraging others to participate as well. In addition to teaching them about the importance of participation in group work, it can be helpful to set up systems and structures that require all students to participate.

We often see group work organized such that each student has a role. One student might be assigned to be the recorder; another, the facilitator; another, the questioner; and the fourth, the timekeeper. Unfortunately, all too often, it is the English language learner, the student who may be most in need of language practice, who is assigned the role of timekeeper—a role that requires little or no language and certainly no interaction with the content. Moreover, it is not even a necessary role; as we've already noted, there are other ways to help students manage their time. This is not to say that students should never be assigned roles. In Chapter 3, we saw Mr. Barber assign roles quite effectively when his students were first learning to do reciprocal teaching. The difference is that in that case, each role is equally important in making meaning. Mr. Barber's expectation is also that students will practice all roles and eventually, as they become more comfortable with the process, will no longer need to be assigned roles.

One way of assuring that all students participate and learn is a collaborative structure called "numbered heads together" (Kagan, 1992). Each group is assigned a number, and each student within the group is assigned a number from 1 to 4 (or 5 when the numbers don't work out evenly to 4). The teacher asks a question and tells students to make sure every student in the group can answer the question. After a predetermined amount of time, usually a minute or two or more, the teacher spins the overhead spinner and announces the number of the student who must answer, perhaps number 3. Groups then have one more minute to make sure that student number 3 in their group can answer the question. The teacher spins again and announces the number of the group that must respond. In this way, students support each other to make sure they all can answer because they never know who will be called on. This strategy is most effective when groups earn points for correct responses.

The other major problem with assigning roles is that only one student is the writer. We prefer to see that all students are required to write their own copies, whether of notes, a skit, or a graphic organizer. Obviously, when the task is to create a poster, this is not so simple. Later in this chapter, you will see how Ms. Chang builds in accountability as her students create a collaborative poster. Each student in the group selects a different colored pen, and all colors must appear on the poster in relatively equal amounts. (She uses this meaning of equality as an opportunity to reinforce understanding of percentage in her math class.) Ms. Chang also insists that, regardless of who is the best artist or who has the best handwriting in the group, all must do both writing and drawing on the poster.

Once we've resolved the issue of all students contributing to the creation of the product, we are left with the question of how to ensure that all students contribute to its presentation. Even when students have written a dialogue—say, to represent the main ideas and events of the westward movement—it may not have a part for all four students. Because we want all our students to practice speaking in more formal situations, we ask that all students present the dialogue even if it means that two students will recite one part chorally. If they are presenting a poster, we give them time to determine how they will organize their presentation so that all group members play an equally important role.

## Managing Cultural Diversity

Another challenge to managing effective group work can be norms of behavior, whether they are individual differences in personality or more general differences in cultural practices. In some cultures it is considered inappropriate for boys and girls to work together. Students from other cultures may be used to working independently and may be uncomfortable working in a group. Because we live in a society where people work together at some point in virtually all careers and walks of life, it is important for students to be able to step outside this comfort zone and engage in whatever configuration they may find themselves. Teaching students to participate effectively while still recognizing, valuing, and allowing for these differences can be a delicate balance. As we create an environment that fosters teamwork, we can hold frank discussions about cultural and personal differences and the reasons for learning to work both independently and collaboratively. We can also vary the structures for learning, sometimes grouping girls with girls and boys with boys, for example. And for those students who prefer to work independently, we can negotiate with them, allowing them to work independently for part of a project or for certain projects and progressively moving them into more collaborative situations.

## Setting Clear Expectations and Outcomes

In Chapter 3, we discussed the importance of making the purpose of each lesson clear to students in order to focus their attention and help to build schemas and understanding. Setting clear expectations and outcomes is also an important factor in managing group work effectively. Many of us have had the unfortunate experience of designing what we thought was an exciting and interesting collaborative task for our students, only to watch it go over like the proverbial lead balloon. Upon reflection, we may realize that the reason for the failure was not so much the lesson design but that students did not understand what we expected them to do. Asking students to work together is far more complicated than simply assigning the odd-numbered questions at the end of the chapter. It requires making the procedures of the task as well as the expectations for quality and substance of the outcome crystal clear for all students. This may mean showing models of completed work, writing the directions in addition to telling the students what to do, or modeling how to do the task (as we saw with the fishbowl). Posters of the steps involved in each collaborative task are one way of helping students learn what they are supposed to do.

Mr. Lopez, a 2nd grade teacher, and Ms. King, a 10th grade world history teacher, both use the same procedures to make sure students know what the assignment is. They write the steps of the task on an overhead or chart, tell the students what they will be doing, and then ask a student to tell the class what the first step is. They then ask another student to tell the class what the first student said. This repetition encourages all students to listen and has the added benefit for English language learners, who may have difficulty in comprehending multistep directions, of giving them multiple opportunities to hear the directions.

## Managing Talk in Pairs

Partner talk is the bread and butter of a classroom filled with the talk of learning. Teachers most commonly invite students to "turn to a partner" to discuss the topic of the moment. As noted in Chapter 4, this simple partner-talk method should be used frequently to allow students lots of opportunities to apply new learning. But work accomplished in pairs is also done during collaborative learning activities designed to move students to an increased level of independence.

### Busy Bees

In Chapter 3, kindergarten teacher Mr. Velez used the "busy bees" strategy to foster partner talk with his students as they shared their opinions about a recent visit to the zoo. This activity is suitable for children in kindergarten through 2nd grade. The teacher introduces the activity by explaining how bumblebees fly. The children, who are on their feet, mimic the buzzing sound and slow movement of bumblebees as they buzz around the room. With an announcement from the teacher of "Busy bees, fly!" the students shuffle their feet and buzz until they hear, "Busy bees, land!" The "bee" they are standing next to becomes their partner for a brief learning activity. For example, 1st grade teacher Ms. Tyler gives each of her students a few math cubes to hold in one hand, along with a sheet of paper and pencil attached to a clipboard. With each "landing," the partners add the total number of cubes and write an addition problem on their papers. Ms. Tyler uses this activity in place of math drill worksheets to provide practice for her students.

### Walking Review

Busy bees is not developmentally appropriate for older students, but a walking review accomplishes similar goals. Like the "Find Someone Who ..." handout used for students to get to know one another, this activity is an excellent replacement for completing independent worksheets and for reviewing material. Each student in the class has a worksheet to be completed and is given a limited period of time to find someone else in the class who can answer each question. Students sign their names next to each answer they log onto someone else's worksheet, and no one can provide more than one answer on any given paper. The goal of this activity is to encourage students to speak to as many classmates as possible about the concepts under review.

Mr. Clark uses walking reviews every Friday in his 8th grade science class to review the week's lessons on chemical reactions. "This is a great way for me to use some of the worksheet materials that come with the textbook program," he explains. He sets the timer for 10 minutes and moves among the students as they roam the room looking for peers who can answer each question. To provide his English language learners with the support they need to approach fellow classmates, he meets briefly with those who need it to give them questions to ask (e.g., "Do you know the answer to number 3?"). When he has students who are very new to English, he partners them with another student to walk the room. "I get a really good sense of who knows something and who doesn't," he says. Mr. Clark asks students to complete the last question on the paper independently back at their desks. "As they all drift back to their seats, the room gets quieter, and I can gauge how much more time might be needed. And don't forget, it gets everyone back in their seats!"

## Explorers and Settlers

As with busy bees and walking review, this instructional routine also requires students to move about the room. However, this approach offers a bit more crowd control because only half of the students are in motion. The teacher begins by reminding students about the differences between explorers, who sought out new lands, and settlers, who cultivated the land and built permanent communities. Assign half of the students to the role of explorers (a good way is to divide the alphabet by last name), and explain that they will seek out settlers to discuss a question.

Ms. Lee does this activity in a rotation of three or four discussion prompts in her 5th grade social studies class. After assigning the roles, she posts the following prompts on the board:

- Discuss the ways of life of the Pueblo Indians of the Southwest.
- Discuss the ways of life of the woodland peoples of the East.
- What did these two groups have in common?
- How did geography influence their different ways of life?

Ms. Lee used a countdown timer for each question so that the partners could monitor their discussion. As the timer approached zero, she invited the explorers to find a new settler and directed them to the next question.

There are variations of the explorers/settlers theme, including couch potatoes/aerobics instructors (physical education), electrons/protons (science), and carriers/borrowers (mathematics). Purposefully planning when using this strategy can scaffold language for students who are learning English. You can, for instance, assign students at early levels of proficiency to be explorers and then assign the settlers to be the first ones to speak. This approach provides an opportunity for English language learners to hear the language of other more proficient students and rehearse what they might say before they have to speak. When you ask them to repeat the process, it provides multiple opportunities for them to hear and use language related to the same question.

### Inside/Outside Circles

In Chapter 3, Ms. Schmidt used inside/outside circles during her lesson in her 5th grade social studies class. This strategy also requires student movement and is intended to extend thinking through multiple conversations. Two concentric circles of students stand and face one another. The teacher poses a question to the class, and the partners talk for a brief time (usually 30–60 seconds). At the signal, the outer circle rotates one position to the left to face a new partner. The conversation continues for several rotations.

Mr. Garland uses inside/outside circles in his 10th grade English class to get discussion going about a thought-provoking question. "You've got to ask a good, meaty question," he cautions, "or they'll run out of things to say pretty quickly." His class will be reading a variety of titles to explore the essential question "When does the desire to obtain something or someone become destructive?" For several minutes, students explore this idea with a series of partners, while Mr. Garland listens in on the conversations. "It helps me to make connections to books I am going to discuss with them, and reminds me of what's in the heads of 15-year-olds."

### Barrier Games

Much of what students are required to do in school is performance driven—solving math problems, completing science labs, and the like. A tremendous amount of academic discourse is needed to do such tasks, but English language learners sometimes rely on other methods of communication, such as gestures, to substitute for technical vocabulary. Barrier games are joint tasks completed by partners who have an obstruction blocking their field of view. For them to succeed, they must rely on clear communication and precise vocabulary. Here are some examples of barrier games:

- Sequencing a set of pictures in the correct order to illustrate the steps to making and glazing a ceramic pot
- Giving a partner directions to draw the life cycle of a butterfly

- Describing the difference between two similar illustrations of molecules
- Solving a crossword puzzle where each partner has half of the clues

Mr. Dare requires the students in his woodshop class to be able to correctly name each type of equipment used in the class. He assigns partners and places a low cardboard shield on the desk so that they cannot see the cards the other holds. One partner has an unlabeled photograph of a piece of shop equipment, while the other has written descriptions of each. The partners work together to describe and match each photo with its correct name and purpose. Only after students have completed this task are they allowed to operate any of the equipment.

## Managing Talk in Groups

Some instructional tasks require the give-and-take of a slightly larger group of students. Collaborative learning among four students is a bit more active than partner activities, so the noise meter is useful when setting up these tasks. In addition, group tasks tend to be a bit longer than those accomplished in pairs, so a display of elapsed time gives students a way of monitoring their progress and adjusting their rate of work.

### Collaborative Posters

A jointly produced final product is useful for group tasks because it gives all the members a shared focus. However, a common problem is that these tasks often fall to one member who does all the writing (and, therefore, much of the thinking). An easy solution is the collaborative poster discussed earlier in this chapter, where each member of the group is given a pen of a different color and all sign their names accordingly.

Ms. Chang uses collaborative posters in her geometry class to get academic discourse and technical vocabulary going. Each group uses theorems to analyze an equation and produce a proof. As Ms. Chang circulates among the groups, she can immediately evaluate the level of participation within the groups and offer extra support to those who do not seem to be sharing their ideas as effectively.

## Jigsaw

This instructional routine was developed by Eliot Aronson in the 1970s to support the efforts of a recently desegregated elementary school in Texas. The original intent was to foster cooperation among students who did not associate much with one another, but Aronson (2000) and his graduate students quickly learned of the academic benefits to this approach. Each student in the class has two memberships: a home group and an expert group. Each home group of four members meets to discuss the task and divide the work according to the teacher's directions. For example, a long reading might be divided into sections. After each home group member has his or her task, the groups move to expert groups composed of members with the same task. The expert groups meet to read and discuss their portion of the assignment and practice how they will teach it when they return to their home groups. Once together again, each student teaches his or her portion of the task to fellow home group members and learns about the other sections of the reading.

Jigsaws are also useful for creating discussions. Ms. Armstrong has been reading aloud the book *Holes* (Sachar, 1998) to her 4th grade students for the last two weeks. After creating home groups of four students, she tells them to decide who will become an expert on each of the following questions:

- In what ways does Stanley Yelnats change throughout the story? Is he a better person?
- Is Stanley a hero, or is he just a person who makes good choices? What's the difference?
- Why do you think the author entitled this book *Holes*?
- Do you think that the Yelnats family's bad luck was due to a curse or something else?

Ms. Armstrong's students joined expert groups to discuss their assigned question at length and debate various ideas raised during the conversations. After 15 minutes, they rejoined their home groups to discuss all four of the questions as each member took a turn facilitating the dialogue.

## Managing Listening, Speaking, Reading, Writing, and Thinking

Although the focus of this book is oral discourse in the classroom, we are reminded that oracy and literacy are inextricably intertwined. We use talk to prepare students before they read or write, to enhance comprehension and improve writing, and to encourage reflection and self-monitoring after reading or writing. Perhaps most important, we use talk as a means of engaging students in high levels of critical thinking. As we saw in Chapter 3, opportunities for talk are continuously and seamlessly integrated into opportunities to read, write, and think. Let's take a look inside Ms. Zamorano's 1st grade classroom to see how her students engage in listening, speaking, reading, writing, and thinking.

### Language Experience Approach

It's October, and hurricane season is just ending. Ms. Zamorano's students have been learning about weather and how it affects the way people live. While part of the class is working in pairs to write a description of what happens during a hurricane, Ms. Zamorano pulls a small group of English language learners aside for a language experience activity. These are students at fairly early levels of proficiency who mostly speak in short phrases or sentences.

The students begin by looking at a picture of a tree-lined street along the beach. The wind is blowing, the waves are large, one tree lies across the street, and a man and a boy hold hands as they cross the street. Ms. Zamorano asks the students to think for a minute about what they see in the picture, what has just happened, what is happening now, and what they think will happen next. She sets up her questions to elicit vocabulary as well as to teach and practice present, past, and future verb tenses. Together, partners tell each other what they see in the picture. Some students are speaking in isolated words ("Man," "Boy," "Tree"); others string their words together in short phrases ("Tree fall down," "Two people run"). Each student is able to participate at his or her own level of language. Ms. Zamorano draws a circle in the middle of a piece of chart paper and writes the word *hurricane* in the circle. Then, as the children share what they see in the picture, she writes their words around the circle, grouping the words in categories of things, actions, and feelings. The students practice the pronunciation of the words with Ms. Zamorano, and then they work with their partners to make sentences using the words.

As students share aloud their sentences, Ms. Zamorano writes them on the chart. Although she uses their language, she does model correct grammar, asking students' permission before she writes the revised sentence and then asking students to say each sentence with her. She helps them expand their sentences by asking questions to elicit more detail. Because she wants them to write a narrative, she guides them to group the sentences that fit together and then to sequence them chronologically. On another chart, she rewrites the sentences into the sequence the students have chosen. They read the paragraph aloud and then copy it into their journals. Later, during learning center time, they will reread the paragraphs, cut the paragraphs into sentences and the sentences into words, and then put them back together. The sentences are also used for practice in changing verb tense or adding different sensory words. The paragraphs are collected into a book for students to read during independent reading.

The beauty of the language experience approach is that it uses the students' own language and thinking to expand their language and thinking. Students learn to read and write what they can say and understand. They add to the language they already know. It can be used at any grade level, with students of any proficiency level, as a way to model and guide writing about any topic in any genre or discipline.

## Summary

Although the management associated with promoting talk in the classroom can be significant, it is well worth the investment. If students are to benefit from the academic discourse, they must become practiced in engaging in it outside the direct supervision of the teacher. This means that the tasks must be organized and have a clearly stated purpose. In addition, the tasks themselves must be sufficiently interesting so that students will want to invest their time. The collaborative learning that occurs in classrooms rich in talk most closely mirrors the kinds of conversations that will dominate students' postsecondary lives. It seems that it is never too early, or too late, to foster language among learners.

# Assessments of Classroom Talk

As her 7th grade science students complete their collaborative tasks, Ms. Barlow meets with a group of them for guided instruction. The focus of the class is on the joints of the body (wrist, shoulder, thigh) and how these are similar to and different from structures used in machines and simple devices (hinge, ball-and-socket, and sliding joints). In terms of language goals, the class has been working on classifying, comparing, and contrasting. The five students meeting with Ms. Barlow are discussing the simple machines lab that they had done the day before. As part of the lab, they had to analyze the ways that several old objects operate. These "antiques" included mason jars, barn pulleys, hand grinders, sewing scissors, Winchester screwdrivers, irons that were heated on the stove, cream and egg beaters, and pump handles. Ms. Barlow had collected these items from garage sales in her neighborhood and knew that her students hadn't seen most of them and thus couldn't really name them. They had to focus on the ways in which these simple machines worked. As she sits with these students, Ms. Barlow collects very important assessment information. Here's part of their conversation:

**Javier:** In our classification, we put the hinge things in categories.

**Ms. Barlow:** You had more than one category for *hinged* items?

**Javier:** No, we made the hinged things one categories.

**Ms. Barlow:** Hmm, I guess I'm confused. I understand that there were several *hinged items*, but did you put them in one *category* or several *categories*?

**Javier:** Oh, just one category for all of the hinged stuff. We put them all in one. This one, for the door, and the scissors.

**Thuy:** Is it wrong? We could do again.

**Ms. Barlow:** Oh, no, I didn't mean it was wrong. I just was trying to understand what you did and how your brains worked. You don't need to do the lab again.

**Thuy:** We also make classification for levers [pronounced "lee-vers"].

**Ms. Barlow:** You did? You *made* a category for *levers*? What items did you place in the classification of *levers*?

**Thuy:** We put screwdriver this classification.

**Maria:** And also the thing that you could pull up and down like this [demonstrates a handle moving].

**Ms. Barlow:** The pump handle?

**Maria:** What is pump?

**Ms. Barlow:** Well, the pump handle was used to get water out of the ground. It was placed over a well, a source of water in the ground.

Consider all of the information Ms. Barlow has gathered in this very brief exchange. She knows that Javier understands the content but needs to spend more attention on plurals and adjective agreement. She provides him with some modeling to determine whether he notices the errors and corrects them, which he does. She also knows that Thuy understands the content but has difficulty with pronunciation and grammar—she seems to miss past tense markers, articles, and referents. Ms. Barlow also knows that Maria understands the content and is ready for additional instruction in the area of vocabulary.

In this chapter, we'll focus on the use of assessments useful in developing oracy when guiding instruction. These tools allow teachers to provide needs-based instruction related to talk that will also build students' reading and writing skills.

## Defining Assessment

Assessment is the systematic process of collecting information about performance. Of course, there are all kinds of ways to assess performance. Formal assessment measures include standardized tests, standards-based tests, and criterion-referenced tests. Each of these tests has expected performance levels that can be used to compare a specific student's achievement with a larger sample or criteria.

Assessment is more than just testing. As educators, we use testing for state accountability purposes. Such tests have limited ability to guide instruction, often because the results are not immediately available. Most teachers use informal assessments to guide instruction and monitor progress. Informal assessments include observations, portfolios, checklists, inventories, rubrics, surveys, conferences, and self-assessments.

## Purposes of Assessment

There are four major reasons for assessment:

1. To determine the skills that a student does and does not have (rubrics, checklists)
2. To guide instructional interventions for improving performance (observations, interviews, checklists, inventories, self-assessments)
3. To monitor development and progress over time and determine what was learned after instruction (performance events, tests)
4. To identify a need for special services (home language surveys, hearing screenings)

In this chapter, we will focus on formative assessments that can be used to change student performance such that the outcomes on a summative assessment are positive. Our experience with English language learners suggests that teachers need to regularly monitor progress and plan instruction based on both content and language expectations if these students are to make progress (Fisher, 2005; Fisher & Frey, 2007).

## Talking Assessments That Guide Instruction

Although measuring talk in the classroom is the ultimate performance assessment, many teachers report discomfort with their ability to do so (Oliver, Haig, & Rochecouste, 2005). This is likely due to the transient nature of the product (speech), which makes assessing it more complicated than assessing writing, which is permanent. Additional reasons for the dearth of oral language assessments in classrooms include concerns that assessment implies judgment of a child's identity and a curricular bias toward written work over discourse. When oral language *is* assessed, it is almost exclusively during formal presentations (Oliver et al., 2005).

The fleeting nature of speech makes assessment tools all the more necessary, as it is difficult to accurately describe student oracy without them. Parents, fellow teachers, and the students themselves want and need useful information about language growth. Issues of language and identity are also important to acknowledge. Although we appreciate that teachers are often reluctant to place value judgments on students' language, we believe that such reluctance is ultimately misguided. Recall the discussion in Chapter 2 regarding language registers. As educators, our goal is to open the world to our students. In terms of language registers, this means expanding their capability to participate in the discourse of the classroom, which in turn buys them the freedom to live, work, and play according to their own desires.

If oral language assessments are to be useful for monitoring progress and planning instruction and intervention, then they must collectively represent several dimensions of language use. It is essential to measure a student's language use in naturalistic environments as well as during public speaking opportunities in the classroom. Teachers also find it useful to gauge students' semantic knowledge and ability to make themselves understood. Other assessments are helpful for determining what students know and don't know about the grammatical structures of the language. Finally, analysis of student writing can provide insight as to student needs for further instruction and support.

## Oral Language Observation

The most common observational tool for assessing the oral language skills of English language learners is probably the Student Oral Language Observation Matrix (SOLOM), which focuses on five areas of oral language development: comprehension, fluency, vocabulary, pronunciation, and grammar. There are five proficiency levels to this tool (see Figure 6.1), which we have aligned with those identified by the Teachers of English to Speakers of Other Languages.

Typically, teachers observe students in at least three different settings and then identify a global score in each of the five areas. The choice of settings can include whole-class instruction, small-group instruction, an individual interview, playground or social interactions, discussions with family members, or peer group talk. To ensure that student proficiency levels are correctly identified, it's important to observe the students in settings in which language is required.

### Administrating the SOLOM

The SOLOM is an individual, not group, assessment. Observe the student in several different authentic classroom activities in which he or she is interacting with the teacher or classmates, such as cooperative group tasks. Observe for a minimum of 10 minutes on each occasion, and each time mark the rankings on the matrix according to your impressions of the student's use of English. You may wish to create an audio recording of one or more of your sessions to go back

**Figure 6.1**  Student Oral Language Observation Matrix (SOLOM)

Student Name: _____    Grade: _____    Age: _____    Language: _____

| | 1 | 2 | 3 | 4 | 5 | Scores |
|---|---|---|---|---|---|---|
| **Comprehension** | Cannot be said to understand even simple conversation | Has great difficulty following what is said; comprehends only social conversation spoken slowly with frequent repetitions | Understands most of what is said at slower-than-normal speed with repetitions | Understands nearly everything at normal speed, although occasional repetition may be necessary | Understands everyday conversations and normal classroom discussions without difficulty | |
| **Fluency** | Speech is so halting and fragmentary as to make conversation virtually impossible | Usually hesitant; often forced into silence by language limitations | Speech in everyday conversation is somewhat limited because of inadequate vocabulary | Speech in everyday conversation and classroom discussion is generally fluent, with occasional lapses while student searches for the correct manner of expression | Speech in everyday conversation and classroom discussion is fluent and effortless, approximating that of a native speaker | |
| **Vocabulary** | Vocabulary limitations are so extreme as to make conversation virtually impossible | Misuse of words and very limited vocabulary make comprehension quite difficult | Words are often misused; conversation is somewhat limited because of inadequate vocabulary | Occasionally uses inappropriate terms or must rephrase ideas because of lexical inadequacies | Use of vocabulary and idioms approximates that of a native speaker | |
| **Pronunciation** | Pronunciation problems so severe as to make speech virtually unintelligible | Very hard to understand because of pronunciation problems; must frequently repeat in order to be understood | Pronunciation problems require listeners to concentrate and occasionally lead to misunderstanding | Always intelligible, though one is conscious of a definite accent and occasional inappropriate intonation patterns | Pronunciation and intonation approximate that of a native speaker | |
| **Grammar** | Errors in grammar and word order so severe as to make speech virtually unintelligible | Grammar and word errors make comprehension difficult; must often rephrase or restrict speech to basic patterns | Makes frequent errors and uses word order that occasionally obscure meaning | Occasionally makes grammatical or word order errors which do not obscure meaning | Grammatical usage and word order approximates that of a native speaker | |
| **Stages of language development** | Starting<br><br>Score: 20% | Emerging<br><br>Score: 24%–40% | Developing<br><br>Score: 44%–60% | Expanding<br><br>Score: 64%–80% | Bridging<br><br>Score: 84%–100% | TOTAL<br>___ × 4 =<br>___ % |

and confirm your impressions or to look for certain patterns of errors or usage. You will rate the student's language use on a scale from 1 to 5 on each of these traits: comprehension, fluency, vocabulary, pronunciation, and grammar. Cross-check your ratings from the different contexts in which you observed the student for inconsistencies or variations that may indicate different levels of proficiency according to language function or purpose.

## A SOLOM Example

Mr. Phillips, a primary school teacher, uses the SOLOM to determine the type of instruction that English language learners in his class need. He summarizes the use of the SOLOM and his course of action based on the assessment as follows:

> I observed Carlos during three different activities on three different days. I observed him during a language arts group activity, lunch recess, and an art project. Over the three days, Carlos was consistent in his scoring, although I did see a difference while working on academic activities as opposed to nonacademic activities.
>
> For the first assignment, the class was asked to work in groups on depth and complexity icons for our language arts story. Students picked an icon (Details, Rules, Ethics, Language of the Discipline, Across Disciplines, and so on), found examples of that icon in the story, wrote it down, and created a visual representation of that example.
>
> During the course of the assignment, I observed Carlos and focused on his oral language. He sat quietly for most of the project and only spoke when a group member prodded with questions on what he thought they should do and how they should represent their icon (they were working on Past, Present, and Future). In my opinion, it seemed as though the language barrier was affecting Carlos, because he was having a hard time following what his peers were saying. The students in his group did not have a problem understanding him when he spoke, and they genuinely respected his ideas. It just seemed as though Carlos had a hard time keeping

up with the rest of the group's language abilities and had a hard time finding the words to represent his ideas.

For the second observation, I observed Carlos during lunch. We are a small school, and teachers regularly eat with the students in the cafeteria, so students generally act the same whether a teacher is present or not. I observed Carlos laughing and talking in both English and Spanish. He seemed comfortable and confident talking with his friends. The students at the time were telling jokes, and Carlos was able to follow the jokes in English, laughing along with everyone else. He told a joke in Spanish and had another student translate the joke for him. But when the students were talking, he spoke in English. He mispronounced a lot of words, but it didn't seem to bother him or the group of students with whom he was socializing.

The third observation took place during an art project. Right away I noticed that Carlos was not following some of my instructions. The assignment covered depth and perception, and I believe that the vocabulary was a stumbling block for him. He was hearing some words for the first time, and there were no words that he could relate to in the instructions. I gave the students a step-by-step diagram to follow during the project, and Carlos seemed to follow the diagrams just fine. He asked a student in Spanish to clarify the instructions.

According to the SOLOM, overall Carlos is in the "Developing" stage of English language proficiency. He has varying degrees of strength, depending on the activities: his English comprehension is strong during nonacademic activities, but he struggles with academic content. He is able to understand conversations in social settings, but has trouble understanding new vocabulary. Carlos typically does not ask to clarify anything; he seems more content trying to figure it out for himself, although he does occasionally ask another student for clarification.

Fluency is Carlos' weakness; he performs at the "Emerging" level here. In an academic setting, Carlos does not volunteer answers. Although he will answer if called upon, he struggles to find the correct vocabulary with which to do so and speaks haltingly.

Carlos' vocabulary is emerging and developing, but must expand in both academic and nonacademic settings. He will often use two- to three-word sentences when speaking. I have noticed that he does not blurt out answers but rather thinks about what he is going to say and how he is going to say it. In normal conversations, he becomes silent because of his vocabulary.

I and most of the students usually understand what Carlos is trying to pronounce. When he does not say a word correctly, his point is still understood. He is able to get through a conversation without repeating his words.

Based on my findings, I implemented some changes in my classroom to accommodate Carlos' language development needs. I continue to place Carlos in heterogeneous groups, which provide him with a low-anxiety environment that mirrors the security he feels in nonacademic settings. He needs to continue his oral language development. I see that one of his problems is that he is shy or embarrassed about the way he speaks. If I can make him feel comfortable, as he was during the lunch observation, then I think he will develop by using the language more often. In addition, I will schedule more small-group discussions with Carlos so that we can work on vocabulary development. While he has made considerable progress, he needs to build his stores of word knowledge if he is to be successful.

Carlos' SOLOM scores are as follows:

- Comprehension: 3 (Developing)
- Fluency: 2 (Emerging)
- Vocabulary: 3 (Developing)
- Pronunciation: 3 (Developing)
- Grammar: 2 (Emerging)

Obviously, the SOLOM helped Mr. Phillips plan instruction for Carlos. But the SOLOM is typically only administered a few times per year—usually in September, January, and April. It is a formative assessment and provides teachers with overall information about student needs and strengths. Although it is useful for identifying a general proficiency level and gauging progress over time, without listening carefully to the specific vocabulary and language structures that students use, teachers cannot target specific areas to develop.

## Retelling

The SOLOM serves as a quick and easy way to get an idea of general proficiency level. Obtaining more precise information about what language students control and what specific errors students are making requires sitting down with each student and listening carefully to that student's language. Oral retelling is an excellent way to zero in on a student's use of language within the context of any content area. Retelling can be formal—retellings are frequently part of standardized language assessment tools—or informal and can be linked directly to classroom texts and activities. It can also be used as a powerful instructional tool. The process is simple:

1. The teacher reads a short piece of text to the student.
2. The student retells the text.
3. The teacher evaluates the student's retelling.

We believe the most useful information comes from having students retell after engaging in tasks that reflect classroom instruction. In other words, when you read the text to the students, you follow the same sorts of procedures you would typically use in teaching—activating prior knowledge, having students predict from the title, calling attention to and explaining key vocabulary, asking questions to increase comprehension, and so forth. In this way, you can gauge what the student can and cannot do within the classroom environment. At certain points in the year, however, you may want to eliminate the instructional scaffolds in order to determine what the student can do independently. You can also modify the procedure using pictures rather than text. It is most helpful to teach the retelling procedure prior to using it as an assessment. Figure 6.2 compares the steps in teaching students to retell with the steps in conducting retelling as an assessment.

| Figure 6.2 | Retelling Procedures |
| --- | --- |

| Retelling for Instruction | Retelling for Assessment |
| --- | --- |
| 1. Explain what retelling is and why we do it. Give examples of when we retell in everyday life (e.g., telling a friend about a movie). <br> 2. Connect to prior knowledge (e.g., have partners retell their morning from getting up to arriving at school). <br> 3. Model retelling. <br> 4. Conduct a shared retelling: chunk the text, provide visual supports, use a graphic organizer to have students write a summary statement, illustrate, and so forth. <br> 5. Have students practice a retell with a partner. <br> 6. Review what retelling is. <br> 7. Have students reflect on what strategies they use to help them recall the text. | 1. Connect to prior knowledge. <br> 2. Ask student to use the title of the text to predict. <br> 3. Tell the students you will read the text aloud twice and then ask them to tell you, in as much detail as they can, what the text was about and to include their own thinking about it. <br> 4. Provide visual support to help students recall (if your focus is language production rather than on listening comprehension). <br> 5. Ask a student to retell the text. <br> 6. Use prompts as necessary: "Tell me more." "What else do you remember?" <br> 7. Ask questions to elicit skill in summarizing, analyzing, synthesizing, comparing/contrasting, and so forth: "What would you say if you were going to tell a friend in a few words what was the most important thing?" "How would you compare _____ to _____?" |

## How to Evaluate a Retell

As you listen to students retell, you want to listen carefully to what they say and how they say it. Figure 6.3 displays a rubric that describes the components of each of the following three key areas of academic oral language proficiency:

- Content: clarity and organization of ideas, comprehensiveness, and original analysis
- Language and vocabulary: sentence structure, grammar, and academic vocabulary
- Fluency: pronunciation, prosody, and flow

**Figure 6.3    Retelling Rubric**

| Level | Content | Language and Vocabulary | Fluency |
|---|---|---|---|
| Level 5 Bridging | • Clearly identifies main idea<br>• Includes major elements (facts, events, ideas, characters, setting, etc.) of the text<br>• Retells story or text in appropriate sequence or organization<br>• Includes all or most supporting details<br>• Incorporates own thinking (e.g., opinion, connection, inference, etc.) | • Varies sentence structure<br>• Uses complex sentences with appropriate, high-level linking vocabulary (*therefore, although,* etc.)<br>• May have a few minor errors in language structures that do not obscure meaning<br>• Uses subjects and verbs that agree, with only a few minor errors<br>• Makes errors that are primarily in complex structures<br>• Uses appropriate verb tenses<br>• Uses key academic vocabulary from the text<br>• Uses vocabulary that expresses higher-order thinking skills (*compare/contrast* etc.) | • Uses speech that is fluent, without hesitation<br>• Uses speech that approximates that of a native speaker<br>• Uses vocabulary that is precise so that the student is able to express meaning clearly and succinctly |
| Level 4 Expanding | • Identifies main idea<br>• Includes most major elements of the text<br>• Retells story mostly in appropriate sequence or organization<br>• Includes some supporting details<br>• Expresses own thinking when prompted | • Varies sentence structure somewhat<br>• Uses some complex sentences with appropriate, simple linking vocabulary (*because, when, first, then,* etc.)<br>• Makes errors in language structure that are mostly minor and do not obscure meaning<br>• Uses subjects and verbs that mostly agree, with minor errors<br>• Uses mostly appropriate verb tenses<br>• Uses most key academic vocabulary from the text<br>• Uses some descriptive vocabulary | • Is usually fluent<br>• Occasionally hesitates while searching for correct expression |

**Figure 6.3**   Retelling Rubric (*continued*)

| Level | Content | Language and Vocabulary | Fluency |
|---|---|---|---|
| Level 3<br>Developing | • Identifies main idea<br>• Includes some major elements of the text<br>• Retells text somewhat in appropriate sequence or logical organization<br>• Includes a few supporting details | • Uses little variation in sentence structure<br>• May use compound sentences with simple linking vocabulary (*and, but,* etc.)<br>• Many errors in language structure that obscure meaning somewhat<br>• Many errors in subject–verb agreement that may obscure meaning slightly<br>• Uses some key academic vocabulary from the text<br>• Uses little descriptive vocabulary | • Is somewhat fluent<br>• Often hesitates while searching for correct expression |
| Level 2<br>Emerging | • Identifies main idea<br>• Includes a few major elements of the text<br>• Retells text without logical organization | • Uses simple sentence structure<br>• May use syntax from native language<br>• Many errors in language structure that obscure meaning significantly<br>• Many errors in subject–verb agreement that obscure meaning significantly<br>• Uses primarily simple present tense<br>• Uses little or no key academic vocabulary<br>• Uses simple, repetitive vocabulary | • Has great difficulty communicating ideas<br>• Is often unable to find correct vocabulary or expression<br>• May use familiar phrases |
| Level 1<br>Entering | • Includes one or two major elements of the text by expressing in single words or pointing to illustrations<br>• May use native language | • May use familiar phrases and patterns of language<br>• Uses incomplete or very simple sentences with major errors that obscure meaning<br>• Is unable to retell text using more than a few isolated words or phrases | • Is very hesitant, may require prompting to speak<br>• Speaks in one- or two-word phrases |

## Speaking Checklist

Teachers use speaking checklists in a number of ways, ranging from formal presentations to extemporaneous speech. In some classrooms, teachers ask students to present to their peers in either small-group or whole-class arrangements. In these classrooms, students have time during class to work on their speeches, receive feedback from their teacher or peers using the checklist, and incorporate this information into their formal presentation. A sample speaking checklist can be found in Figure 6.4.

In some classrooms, teachers ask their students to present information to students in earlier grades. In such cases, the speaking checklist would be completed by the teacher of the younger students and provided to the presenter. At other times, the use of a speaking checklist is much less formal and is conducted on an individual basis. Students may receive feedback on their speaking skills during small-group lessons, class interactions, and even interactions on the playground.

As with other checklists and rubrics, teachers and students should add additional behaviors they wish to observe and expand upon to their checklist. The example in Figure 6.4 can and should be altered according to the reading and writing fluency of a student, the grade level, the goals of instruction, and the content being studied. Accordingly, there are two blank lines so that additional expectations can be easily added.

Students should understand each of the items on the speaking checklist before it is used as a feedback tool. We have found that it is very effective to introduce the speaking checklist and then invite students to use the checklist as we model examples and nonexamples of the elements of good speaking.

## Repeating Words

Repeating words, either in isolation or as part of a group, requires students to complete a number of cognitive processes. First they have

| Figure 6.4 | Speaking Checklist |
|---|---|

Name: _____    Date: _____

| When _____ speaks in a group, he or she: | Score* | Comments |
|---|---|---|
| introduces the topic. | | |
| builds support for the subject. | | |
| remains on topic. | | |
| speaks clearly, pronouncing words so that audience members understand them. | | |
| uses appropriate volume so audience members can hear. | | |
| uses courteous language. | | |
| incorporates vocabulary expected of the content. | | |
| uses correct grammar structures appropriate for the language register. | | |
| speaks at a rate appropriate for the complexity of the information. | | |
| presents in an organized and interesting way. | | |
| maintains listeners' interest. | | |
| answers questions effectively. | | |
| uses gestures, body language, and facial expressions correctly. | | |
| | | |
| | | |

* Score as follows:
5 = Speaker uses this consistently and correctly.
4 = Speaker uses this frequently, with only minor errors or omissions.
3 = Speaker uses this occasionally.
2 = Speaker uses this occasionally but often incorrectly.
1 = No evidence

to listen to the words, then associate meaning with them, and finally engage in the complex action of speaking. Let's consider a few examples of the use of repeating words to assess student performance.

## Pronunciation

Teachers can easily assess pronunciation skills by asking students to repeat a series of words in which sounds change. Consider the ways in which words are pluralized in English. We use three distinct sounds for regular plurals: "s," "z," and "iz." You might try this yourself. Which sounds are used in the following plural words: *dogs, cats, seas, moths, buses, loves, giraffes,* and *witches*? Of course, specific rules exist for pluralization, but English language learners have often not internalized these rules and need instruction to do so. Asking students to pronounce words, either from an oral model or from the printed page, allows you to determine which have been mastered and which have not. Of course, this doesn't mean that we should make students memorize rules, just that they need systematic instruction and lots of examples to achieve automaticity.

For example, Mr. Martin was listening to La-Quoi read during an individual reading conference. He noticed that La-Quoi had difficulty pronouncing "th" and couldn't reliably turn her voice on or off correctly. Most native speakers of English know that the voice is off when we say "th" in the word *think* but on when we say the "th" in the word *the*. Mr. Martin decided that he would schedule additional short conferences with La-Quoi to help her learn when and when not to turn her voice on for "th" sounds.

## Categories

Another use of repetition involves students identifying as many words as they can in a specific category. This exercise allows the teacher to estimate vocabulary schemas and is especially useful when conducted as part of a topical unit of study.

As a general assessment of spoken vocabulary knowledge, 2nd grade teacher Ms. Miller meets with Miguel, shows him a photo of the grocery store near the school, and then asks him to list all of the things he could buy there. Miguel names 34 common grocery items (e.g., bananas, meat, soup) and two that are not commonly sold at grocery stores (tires and computers). From this quick assessment, Ms. Miller knows that Miguel has developed a rather sophisticated English word knowledge related to the community.

In an 8th grade social studies classroom, Ms. Brighton is concerned about Soung's understanding of the U.S. Civil War. As part of their individual conference, Ms. Brighton asks Soung to identify as many words as she can related to Reconstruction. Soung cannot identify any words. Ms. Brighton attempts to expand the topic to determine Soung's knowledge by asking her to name as many words as she can about the Civil War in general. Soung identifies nine words independently, including *North*, *South*, *fight*, *soldier*, and *war*. Armed with this information, Ms. Brighton knows that she has to intervene. She provides Soung with a picture dictionary and a list of general words related to the Civil War, such as *slavery*, *rebellion*, *opposition*, and *cannon*. She asks Soung to create word cards for each of the words that include the word, what it means, an illustration, and a sentence related to the Civil War. Ms. Brighton asks Soung to work on the first 10 word cards so that they can meet the following day to discuss the meaning of the words and how they relate to their unit of study. Ms. Brighton also knows that she has to provide Soung with other opportunities to learn about the Civil War and checks out DVDs, easy-to-read informational books, and Web sites that could help build Soung's background knowledge and vocabulary. This simple assessment revealed a significant need for a student who had previously sat quietly in the classroom, not disturbing anyone but also not learning much.

## Generative Sentences

Another way to assess students' knowledge of vocabulary and grammar is to ask them to place specific words in a specific place in a sentence. This activity requires that students manipulate information in their minds (inner speaking) as they solve the task. Generative sentences can be constructed in a number of ways, depending on what the teacher wants to assess. In general, generative sentences contain a specific word, the required placement of the word, and information about the expected length of the sentence.

Ms. Betts is assessing students' understanding of homophones and asks Marisol to "invent a sentence that is less than eight words long using this version of word [points to *they're*] in the fourth position." When Marisol responds, "It's time for *their* coffee break," Ms. Betts instantly knows that Marisol still needs instruction in this area.

Generative sentences can also provide teachers with an opportunity to assess students' knowledge of language registers and functions. For example, Mr. Smith asks Liam to "create a formal sentence of any length that requests information and contains the word *performance* anywhere in the sentence." Liam successfully completes this task by responding, "I am calling to ask about the length of the performance this evening."

## Cloze Procedures

To create a cloze assessment, the teacher selects a passage of between 100 and 250 words. Typically, the first sentence in the passage is left intact, and then every fifth word from the remaining text is removed. Then, the teacher reads the passage aloud to a student and asks the student to supply the missing words. In our assessment work with English language learners, we mark a correct response to the oral cloze passages if the student provides either the exact replacement of the original word removed from the text or a matching synonym that meets the text's semantic and syntactic context.

The results from the oral cloze procedure provide teachers with clues about instructional needs. For example, if the student is providing nouns where verbs are obviously needed, the teacher will move in one direction. If the student is providing incorrect tense or agreements, the teacher will move in another direction. If the student is providing incorrect words for the concepts, the student may need to pay more attention to academic vocabulary. If the student is providing random words, the teacher knows that the passage is not being understood and that the text is too difficult for the student.

The oral cloze procedure can be used to assess specific language features. For example, a teacher might choose to remove all of the verbs, all of the adjectives, or all of the prepositions from a passage to determine a student's ability to supply the missing information.

Information from all of the repeated word assessments discussed in this section can also be used to plan collaborative learning activities in which peers talk with one another using the vocabulary, forms, structures, and registers identified in the assessments as areas of need.

## Reversible Sentences

Another category of oral language assessment, and one that provides teachers with an opportunity to delve deeper into students' understanding of the language, involves reversing words in context to determine meaning. A significant amount of work has been done with reversible sentences to determine where language is localized in the brain. By studying people who have had strokes, researchers are able to determine where in the brain specific tasks are likely to be completed (Davis, 2007). For our purposes, reversible sentences provide an interesting window into the internalized language structure of English language learners. Sometimes, these language structures are based on their first language, and teachers need to understand the differences to provide meaningful instruction. Other times, language structures are faulty, and teachers must provide intervention to correct these misunderstandings. We will consider a number of types of reversible sentences and how they are used for assessment with English language learners.

### Possessives

In our oral language assessments of English language learners, we like to start with reversible possessives. Using photographs, magazine cutouts, or illustrations, we ask students to indicate which picture is correct based on the phrase used. We typically start with phrases that are nonsense one way and understandable the other way (e.g., "the cat's food" versus "the food's cat"). English learners at early stages of language proficiency will often select the incorrect phrase, because the translation may work in their home language. In an assessment situation, students will need to complete several of these exercises to ensure that they aren't just making lucky guesses.

If students do well on these types of reversible possessives, we move to plausible reversible possessive sentences in which both could be correct. For example, the student might be shown a photo of a large ship and be asked which is correct: "The ship's captain" or "the captain's ship." As the assessment progresses, students can be asked to identify which picture correctly matches each of the phrases. For example, students might be shown two illustrations and asked to match the following phrases with them: "the cat's owner" and "the owner's cat."

## Agents

Another area of reversible sentences focuses on the agent in the sentence. Again, we can present students with plausible and nonplausible sentences. We typically start with nonplausible to determine whether students understand the role of the agent in an English sentence. For example, again looking at a picture, students might be asked to determine which is correct: "The dog ate my homework" or "The homework ate my dog." This may seem like a very easy task for most students, but English language learners who are accustomed to waiting until the end of a sentence to find out the agent are likely to select the wrong response. The application of rules or expectations from the first language to the second language is known as a *transfer error*, and such mistakes are relatively common yet not often corrected.

In the case of plausible reversible sentences, students are presented with multiple pictures and asked either to match them to the phrase or identify the correct phrase (e.g., "Big Bird is washing Cookie Monster" and "Cookie Monster is washing Big Bird"). Students who select the correct illustrations for these sentences clearly display their understanding of agent and action—an important milestone in English language development. A correct response requires that students successfully negotiate grammar, structure, and vocabulary. Incorrect responses indicate a need for instruction and opportunities for intervention.

## Locatives

The locative is another type of reversible sentence that we like to use in assessments. We reserve this type of assessment for students who have mastered the possessive and agent sentences. Locatives establish where, to where, or from where a state or action happened or existed. Locatives are critical to understanding English because they provide details. We like to use the locative sentences developed by O'Grady, Yamashita, and Lee (2005) in our assessments because they provide a good starting point to determine students' understanding. Their five sentences that require student action are as follows:

- Put the paper on the binder.
- Put the binder on the book.
- Place the Christmas card on the book.
- Drop the paper on the book.
- Drop the book on the binder.

If students cannot correctly follow the instructions of the above sentences, instruction and subsequent assessment in locatives are necessary. If they don't experience difficulty, they don't need instruction in this area. Far too often, English language learners receive instruction in language structures they don't need. Not only does this waste valuable learning time, but it also prevents students from receiving the instruction they do need to progress in English language development.

## Passives

A final type of reversible sentence is the passive one. Passive sentences are difficult for English language learners to understand. The challenge is due to their relative rarity in conversation and in most elementary and middle school reading materials and is complicated by the availability of passive sentences in the home language; for example, Mandarin speakers construct the passive voice by adding a prefix to the active noun phrase and rearranging the word order.

Consider the following two sentences: "She did not drink the milk" and "The milk was not drunk by her." As a fluent reader, you know that both sentences mean the same thing. You probably are somewhat bothered by Sentence B because we've all been taught to avoid the passive voice. In fact, our word-processing software is programmed to tell us that this construction is in error. But passive voice is not ungrammatical. It's a form of language that serves a purpose. Yes, active voice is considered more correct in many cases, but passive voice must be understood. It is used often in academic writing, for example, as it implies a sense of objective distance from the topic, and can also be used to soften a blow in other contexts (e.g., "Your request has been denied" versus "I [or We] denied your request").

## Summary

The use of formative assessments is critical if we are to increase precision in our teaching. English language learners have "double the work" in school because they must simultaneously learn the content and the language. When teachers assess both language and content, students receive instruction that is tailored to their needs.

# Conclusion

The leap from reading about academic discourse to making it an everyday reality can be significant, and we have certainly had our share of good intentions that fizzled. The competing demands of new initiatives and the continuation of existing ones can make all of us feel as though there's no time to squeeze one more thing into our overstuffed curriculum. With these challenges in mind, let's discuss some of the practicalities associated with increasing the quantity and quality of talk in your classroom.

## Setting the Stage for Purposeful Talk

Take stock of the physical space of the classroom: does it invite discussion, or does it isolate? As noted in Chapter 4, the environment transmits our expectations. Ideally, students are able to sit around tables or at desks grouped to face one another. This promotes eye contact and allows students to see the facial expressions and gestures used by others. Consider as well your ability to move around the room so that students can see you. Sight lines are essential, and when you are able to use many parts of the room, you make it easier for your students to track you.

In addition, post visual reminders for students to use during discussions. Prepare posters for the linguistic frames you will be modeling for your students, such as the ones found in Figure 5.2. Other posters can be used to support the habits introduced, such as the accountable talk sentence starters in Figure 5.3. That way they will be available for you to use when a student is at a loss for words. These frames and sentence starters can even be reproduced as table tents, making them convenient prompts for use during small-group discussions.

## Getting Students to Talk

The best way to get students talking is to carefully model what you want them to do. As discussed in Chapter 3, modeling allows you to demonstrate how language is used within the content being taught. Modeling includes sharing your own thinking, so it is important that you take time to reflect on your own processes, since most of us are not in the practice of spontaneously summoning them up. We find it useful to make notes written in the first person on self-sticking notes in advance of our lesson and then affix them to the reading material we're using. Modeling can be further extended for older students, who benefit from your explanations about your teaching as it encourages their growing metacognitive awareness. Tell them why you are modeling ("It helps to hear what's going on in my head so that you can recognize your own thinking").

## What to Do If No One Talks

As teachers, we have become accustomed to dreading the silence that hangs in the air when no one volunteers to reply to a query. Maybe we're all permanently scarred by the science teacher in the movie *Ferris Bueller's Day Off* who would ask, "Anyone? Anyone?" and then go on to answer his own questions when no one replied. When the silence hangs, take a deep breath and wait. We all know about the importance of wait time after posing a question; English language learners need more, especially if they are code switching in their brains as they translate between English and their first language. What is less widely known is that Wait Time II, the pause created by the teacher after a student replies, is even more influential in eliciting more complex language (Tobin, 1987). Develop a habit of counting to yourself after a student answers, and notice whether she adds more to her reply when given the opportunity. It is ironic that the best tool when faced with silence is silence. However, when learners understand that you're willing to create space for them to think, they will reward you with extended responses that are richer and more complex.

## What to Do If Everyone Talks

Even after teaching for so many years, we're still surprised how quickly our students go from the silence of the first day of school to the clamor of a sports event a short week or two later! Anticipate the management they'll need by planning your procedures for time and noise. Chapter 5 contains several ideas for doing so, such as creating a noise meter (Figure 5.4) and using a timer that will cue students when it is time to finish their discussion. When used consistently, these routines catch on quickly and prevent the discourse from devolving into chaos.

## Making Sure Talk Is Productive

Throughout the book we have shared a host of instructional strategies for fostering academic discourse. However, there needs to be more than simply causing talk—students need explicit instruction on the language demands of the task as well. We've included an appendix at the end of this book that pairs each of the instructional strategies we've discussed with examples of the linguistic frames your students will need to apply higher levels of academic language. Use these frames and develop your own to reflect the developmental and language levels of your students, and then remember to model their use. Post these frames as visual reminders, and point out their use during discussions.

## Making Sure That Students Are Making Progress

The last element necessary to move from page to stage is to plan your assessments as carefully as you plan your lessons. Checking for understanding involves more than asking questions; it requires an approach that combines formative assessments with the summative ones that come at the end of the unit. A range of assessments is discussed in Chapter 6, and these should be considered in terms of what they can offer to the overall assessment map of your classroom. For example, the Student Oral Language Observation Matrix (Figure 6.1) could be used at the beginning, middle, and end of the year. These results allow you to understand the developmental stages of language development among your students. In contrast, generative sentences can occur near the end of a lesson introducing new vocabulary or concepts because it gives you immediate feedback on what may need to be retaught. Other assessments such as anticipation guides and cloze passages provide information on what is known at the beginning of a unit of instruction and can reveal gaps in background knowledge as well as areas of prior learning.

## Final Thoughts

No classroom will change overnight from one dominated by teacher talk to one that is filled with high levels of academic discourse. After all, in many cases our students arrive at our doors with years of experience remaining quiet while the teacher does all the work. This scenario is all the more complicated for students who are learning a new language as they simultaneously try to learn the content as well. Like all other aspects of learning, it takes time, repetition, and scaffolded instruction for them to learn how to engage in sophisticated classroom discussions. However, these skills can be taught and honed through the purposeful instruction that comes from planning and assessing. In addition, these skills are further enhanced when the physical, psychological, and social environments are engineered to meet the needs of students. We are ever mindful of James Britton's observation that "reading and writing float on a sea of talk." Under the skilled guidance of a teacher who understands the relationship between language and learning, that sea of talk carries everyone to new learning destinations.

# Appendix: List of Instructional Routines

Explain and model each routine. Post a chart of routines and relevant procedures and linguistic frames, and add to it as students learn new routines. This chart contains samples that may help in creating additional frames to provide language support to discuss the content.

| Strategy | Procedures | Focus on English Language Learners | Linguistic Frames |
|---|---|---|---|
| Anticipation guide | Students agree or disagree with a series of statements written to access and activate their prior knowledge. Statements relate to key concepts, include the likelihood of differing opinions, and should provoke discussion and interest, even controversy. They read the statements individually and then discuss with a partner, come to consensus, and write a statement explaining their rationale. They revisit the guide at the end of the unit or lesson to note any changes in their thinking. At this time, they may write a statement explaining the change in their thinking and cite evidence from the text. | • Be sure to include content with which students have some familiarity so they will experience success.<br>• When the focus is on the content, keep the language and vocabulary at a comprehensible level.<br>• Use some of the new vocabulary with enough context in the statement so that students will understand it. | • I think it's ____ because ____.<br>• I agree/disagree with you because ____.<br>• We both think that ____ because ____.<br>• Why do you think ____?<br>• I believe that ____.<br>• I agree with you up to a point, but I think that ____.<br>• I am willing to change my answer because ____. |
| Barrier games | One partner has a picture or information that the other partner does not have. Students sit back-to-back or have a visual obstruction to block their view (barrier). Using oral language only, students communicate to complete the task. Tasks may require partners to draw a picture, place objects in specific positions, find the difference in two pictures, etc. Students in small groups might each have one picture in a sequence. Without looking at the other pictures, they must put them all in the correct order. | • Good for all levels of English language learners (ELLs).<br>• Use to practice survival vocabulary—food, body, clothing, school items, etc.<br>• Use to reinforce concepts (e.g., pictures of the life cycle of a butterfly).<br>• Use to practice language structures (prepositions, sequence words, etc.).<br>• Teach vocabulary students will need to complete the task. | • I see a ____.<br>• Do you have a ____?<br>• First you (draw, put, place, etc.).<br>• I think ____ (my/your/her/his) picture goes ____ (first, second, next, last) because ____.<br>• There is a ____ (prepositional phrase—on top of, in between, etc.) the ____. |

| | Description | Adaptations | Sentence frames |
|---|---|---|---|
| Busy bees | Students mimic the buzzing sound and slow movement of bumblebees as they buzz around the room to find a partner. Teacher says, "Busy bees, fly!" Students move around the room and buzz until they hear, "Busy bees, land!" The "bee" they are standing next to becomes their partner for a brief learning activity such as giving an opinion or answering a question. | • Pair ELL bees purposefully by giving them different-colored cards—they must find a partner with another color.<br>• Change the color each time you do it, so children cannot easily identify ELLS.<br>• Teach students expected behaviors such as looking at the person talking.<br>• Do not ask students to touch unless you know touching is acceptable in their culture. | • My favorite _____ is _____.<br>• What is your favorite _____?<br>• I think that _____.<br>• I think the funniest part was when _____.<br>• I liked _____ the best because _____. |
| Collaborative dialogue | In groups, students write a dialogue pertaining to the topic. Characters may be human or not (e.g., rational and irrational numbers discussing why they can't get along). The focus of the dialogue should highlight and extend understanding of the main idea of the topic. Students must use the assigned vocabulary. All students write their own copy of the complete dialogue. All students participate in an oral presentation of the dialogue, regardless of the number of characters or students in the group. They may read chorally, take turns playing a role, or find another way for all to participate. It is best to assign different "characters," parts, or prompts to different groups to divide the text or concept and maintain student interest in the presentations. | • Group students heterogeneously.<br>• Give think time so ELLs have time to think about what they will contribute.<br>• ELLs should have an equal or nearly equal part.<br>• Students at early levels of proficiency might read a part chorally with another student.<br>• Give rehearsal time before asking ELLs to perform in front of the class. | • I think we should have the characters _____ (verb).<br>• The setting could be in _____.<br>• First one character can say _____.<br>• Then another character can say _____.<br>• How about if we _____?<br>• I think we should have _____ (character) say _____. |

| Strategy | Procedures | Focus on English Language Learners | Linguistic Frames |
|---|---|---|---|
| Collaborative poster | In groups, students create a poster representing the main ideas of the concept. Give students a rubric that describes what must be included in the poster. After thinking individually about how to represent their ideas, each student selects one color of pen and uses only that color on the chart. All students must contribute to both writing and drawing on the poster and sign it. Display posters in the room. Students evaluate their own poster and at least one other according to the rubric. | • If students present their posters to the class, be sure ELLs participate in the presentation.<br>• Requiring the use of key vocabulary provides an additional opportunity to practice.<br>• Encourage students to talk first and then write and draw. | • I think we should ____.<br>• I can write/draw the ____.<br>• I think that ____ would be a good symbol because it represents ____.<br>• Where should we put the ____?<br>• I like your idea about ____. |
| Coming to consensus | Students in a group share their individual ideas and come to consensus on one common idea to share with the whole group. | • Some ELLs may come from cultures where males are leaders or consensus is an unfamiliar notion.<br>• Be sure that everyone in the group has a voice. | • I like ____'s idea because ____.<br>• I prefer ____'s idea because ____.<br>• I agree that ____ because ____.<br>• I agree with you up to a point, but I think that ____. |

| | | |
|---|---|---|
| Concept sort | Similar to a word sort, students sort single words, phrases, or sentences into categories that relate to the concept they are studying. Sorting may be by category, sequence, characteristics, etc. | • Be sure that ELLs know the vocabulary being used so they can focus on their understanding of the concept.<br>• Manipulating cards is a physical response that can enhance language learning.<br>• Students can copy their sort into a graphic organizer in a notebook. | • I think ____ belongs in this category because ____.<br>• I don't think ____ belongs in this category because it doesn't ____.<br>• ____ should be ____ (first, second, next, last, etc.).<br>• These are different because ____.<br>• These belong in the same category because ____.<br>• What's the difference between ____ and ____? |
| Explorers and settlers | Assign half the students to be explorers and half to be settlers. Explorers seek out a settler to discuss a question. Repeat the process one or two times to discuss the same question or a new, related question. | • Vary the assignment to be an explorer or a settler so that ELLs are not always one or the other.<br>• Assign ELLs at early levels of proficiency to be all explorers or settlers; then have the other group speak first to act as language models. | Sentence frames will vary depending on the prompt and the topic. Samples might include these:<br>• The best thing about ____ is ____.<br>• I still have a question about ____.<br>• I'd like to know more about ____. Can you tell me anything? |

| Strategy | Procedures | Focus on English Language Learners | Linguistic Frames |
|---|---|---|---|
| Find someone who … or Walking review | Students must find a classmate who can answer a question on a handout. They ask the student the question and write down the response they are given and the name of the student who answered. This can be done as a review of learning or in anticipation of learning. It can also be done in the form of a bingo game. | • Have students write down the answer they hear so they practice listening and writing as well as speaking.<br>• ELLs at early levels of proficiency can use a sheet with differentiated questions that address the main idea but use familiar language. | • Do you know _____?<br>• Have you found anyone who _____?<br>• Have you ever _____? |
| Find your partner | Each student is given a card that matches another student's card in some way.<br>• Vocabulary + definition<br>• Question + answer<br>• First half of a sentence + second half<br>• Sentence with a missing word<br>• Math problem with steps to solution<br>• Concept + example<br><br>Variations may be made that require more than two students to form a group:<br>• Steps in a sequence<br>• Items in a category<br>• Sequence of events | • Give clues such as "Look for capital letters and periods to help you find your partner."<br>• Have students read their cards aloud to practice pronunciation.<br>• ELLs at early levels of proficiency can have cards with less or familiar language. | • Do you have something that goes with _____?<br>• My card says _____. What does yours say? |

| | | | |
|---|---|---|---|
| Fishbowl | A group of students models a strategy or task. They sit in the middle of the room (in a "fishbowl"), with remaining students seated around them. Students in the fishbowl engage in the task, with the teacher guiding as needed. Give students outside the fishbowl a purpose for listening. They may complete a graphic organizer, write down a quote or two, listen for specific examples, etc. | • It can be helpful to assign students to focus their listening on one particular student in the fishbowl so they do not get lost in the conversation.<br>• When ELL students are part of the fishbowl, they must be given time to discuss the question or practice the task before they do it in front of the class. | Outside the fishbowl:<br>• I heard _____ say that _____.<br>• After listening to what _____ said, I think that _____.<br>• I have a question about _____.<br>Inside the fishbowl:<br>• Sentence frames will vary depending on the strategy, the prompt, and the topic.<br>• Give ELLs the sentence frames as they discuss in their small group prior to participating in the fishbowl. |
| Four corners | Assign each corner of the room a category related to the topic. Tell the students the four categories and ask them to write down which category they are most interested in, along with two or three reasons for their choice. They then form groups by going to the corner of the room with the category they selected. In groups of three to four students, they share their reasons for their selection. This is also another way to form groups to complete an assigned task. | • Keep group size small so ELLs will have opportunities to participate. | • I chose _____ because _____.<br>• I like _____ because _____.<br>• I chose _____ because I think that _____. |

| Strategy | Procedures | Focus on English Language Learners | Linguistic Frames |
|---|---|---|---|
| Inside/outside circles | Two concentric circles of students stand or sit and face one another. The teacher poses a question to the class, and the partners respond briefly. At the signal, the outer circle rotates one position to the left to face a new partner. The conversation continues for several rotations. For each rotation, students may respond to the same prompt or to a different but related one. | • Vary the circles so that ELLs are not always inside or outside. <br> • Assign all ELLs at early levels of proficiency to inside or outside circles; then have the other circle speak first to act as language models. | Sentence frames will vary depending on the topic and the prompt. Some of the same frames presented in the fishbowl section will work well for inside/outside circles. |
| Interactive lecture | Teacher breaks a lecture (or video) into small segments and gives students processing time after each segment. After each segment, students think, write, talk, or draw about what they have learned or understand. | • Graphic organizers can guide note taking. <br> • Be sure to have students' attention before resuming the lecture—even a few words missed can detract from understanding. | • Sentence frames will vary depending on the topic and the prompt. <br> • Differentiate for students by writing sentence frames on a graphic organizer for those who need them. |
| Jigsaw | Each student in the class has two memberships: a home group and an expert group. Each home group of four members meets to discuss the task and divide the work according to the teacher's directions. After each home group member has a task, they move to expert groups composed of members with the same task. The expert groups meet to read and discuss their portion of the assignment and practice how they will teach it when they return to their home groups. Students teach their expert portion to home group members and learn about the other sections of the reading. | • Assign ELLs with like needs to the same expert group, and provide additional support through differentiated graphic organizers, extra teacher guidance, or even a minilesson. <br> • If expert groups are homogeneous, be sure the task for ELLs provides a high level of challenge and high level of support. | • In our group we learned that _____ and that _____. <br> • Can you explain _____ again? <br> • One important thing about _____ is _____. <br> • What I learned from my expert group was _____. |

| Language experience approach | Students brainstorm words and phrases about a picture or a common experience. The teacher writes words on a chart. Partners create sentences using words. The teacher writes sentences on a chart and then guides the group in organizing sentences into a logical paragraph. Students practice pronunciation and reading aloud and copy the paragraph. Students can write sentences on sentence strips and put the paragraph back together or cut up sentences into words or phrases and put them back together. | • Use students' own language to expand and build upon the vocabulary and structures they already know. <br> • Write student sentences with correct grammatical structures. <br> • This is most effective in a small-group setting to focus the level of language and ensure participation by ELLs at early proficiency levels. | • Because this is direct instruction in constructing sentences, linguistic frames are not needed here. <br> • Sentence frames can be created from the final written product, and students can practice with them in pairs or individually. |
|---|---|---|---|
| Line up | Students line up in a particular order for the purpose of practicing language or getting to know each other, or in a random way to form pairs or groups. Students may line up in order of birthdays, or they may be given cards with information they use to sequence themselves—fraction or percentage cards, sequence of events in a story or history, steps in a process. Once students have formed the line, they may "wrap around," with the student at one end of the line walking down to face the student at the far end of the line, followed by the other students until the line is folded in half with each student facing another. | • This may be done silently, forcing students to use other means of communication besides language. <br> • Beginning ELL students may be paired with another student to support their participation. | • When is your birthday? <br> • I have _____. What do you have? <br> • I think I am _____ (before/after) _____ (you, him, her). <br> • I think my number is _____ (smaller/bigger) than yours because _____. |

| Strategy | Procedures | Focus on English Language Learners | Linguistic Frames |
|---|---|---|---|
| Novel ideas only | Individually, students write down as many items related to the prompt as they can think of. In groups, they take turns sharing one item at a time from their list. Each student must repeat the item mentioned by the previous student before adding a new one. Groups create a list that includes all the items. Each student writes the same list. They draw a line under the last item on the list. Groups stand up; one group reads their list and sits down. All students in the group should participate in reading the list to the class. Other groups add to their list any new items they hear. The next group reads only items that have not been mentioned. Continue in this manner until no group has new items to contribute. | • Have all students participate in reading their list to the class so ELLs can practice language and pronunciation.<br>• Be sure ELLs are not always in the last group to present—the last group typically has little left in their list that has not already been mentioned. | • We already have _____ on our list.<br>• Can you repeat that, please?<br>• I don't have anything new on my list.<br>• Everything on my list has already been mentioned. |
| Numbered heads together | Each group is assigned a number. Each student within the group is assigned (or selects) a number from 1 through 4 (or 5 if numbers necessitate). The teacher asks a question and tells students to make sure every student in the group can answer. After students have time to discuss, the teacher spins an overhead spinner and announces the number of the student. Groups have one more minute to make sure that number student in their group knows the answer. The teacher spins again and announces the number of the group that must respond. | • This provides a structured and supported way to have ELLs respond to whole-class questions.<br>• Have students rehearse with their group what they will say to the class if called on to respond. | • I think you should say _____.<br>• I think the answer is _____.<br>• I'm not sure I know the answer. Is it _____? |

| | | |
|---|---|---|
| Observation charts | Glue pictures to a piece of poster paper, and attach writing paper next to the poster. Pictures should be provocative and stimulate conversation about the topic. Post the charts around the room. Pairs of students move from poster to poster and write<br>• What they observe;<br>• What they think is happening, happened before, or will happen next;<br>• Questions they have. | • This provides visual support to activate prior knowledge.<br>• Captions or labels introduce and reinforce vocabulary. | • I wonder _____ (what/why/when/where/who) _____.<br>• I see _____ and _____.<br>• My observation is that _____. |
| Readers' theater | Students create a script from the story they have read. This is different from a collaborative dialogue in that the events of a narrative are retold in dialogue format. A collaborative dialogue is a conversation that may be related to a text, a concept, a process, etc. | • Require students to use target vocabulary in their script.<br>• Give an opportunity for rehearsal before performing.<br>• Be sure that ELLs have speaking parts equal or nearly equal to those of other students (unless they are at Starting level of proficiency). | • I'd like to be the _____.<br>• My character should say something about _____.<br>• We need to include dialogue about _____. |

| Strategy | Procedures | Focus on English Language Learners | Linguistic Frames |
|---|---|---|---|
| Reciprocal teaching | Students work in groups of four with a common piece of text. Each member has a role: summarizer, questioner, clarifier, or predictor. These roles closely mirror the kinds of reading comprehension strategies necessary for understanding expository text. The reading is chunked into shorter passages so that the group can stop to discuss periodically. | • Teach each role before expecting students to use the entire process.<br>• Provide graphic organizers to take notes.<br>• Have students change roles so that all take on each role with the goal of eventually holding a natural discussion about the text. | • What does ____ mean?<br>• I predict that ____.<br>• In summary, this part is about____.<br>• I'd like to clarify ____. |
| Think-write-pair-share | Give students a minute to *think* about a prompt. Give them a few minutes to *write* down their ideas (typically in bullet or note form without a focus on spelling or grammar). Have students share their ideas in *pairs*. Tell students to listen carefully as they may be asked to share what their partner said. Ask a few pairs to *share* with the whole class. | For very young students or students at early levels of proficiency, it may take too long for them to write their thoughts, so think-pair-share may be a better option. | • I wrote that ____.<br>• When I was ____, I ____.<br>• Let me clarify what I heard you say; you said that ____.<br>• My partner said that ____.<br>• My partner and I both thought that ____. |

| | | | |
|---|---|---|---|
| Three-step interview | Students work first with a partner and then in a group of four to respond to a question. Questions may relate to opinions or be at any level of Bloom's taxonomy. It is helpful to have each pair respond to a different question so that the sharing does not become repetitive and boring:<br>1. Partner A interviews Partner B, while Partner C interviews Partner D.<br>2. Partner B interviews Partner A, while Partner D interviews Partner C.<br>3. Partners A and B tell Partners C and D what their partner said, and Partners C and D tell Partners A and B what their partner said. | • Provide graphic organizers to take notes.<br>• ELLs can interview first so they have a model to follow.<br>• Be sure students have sufficient background knowledge to have information or opinions to share. | • My partner said _____ and _____.<br>• We discussed _____.<br>• We both agreed that _____ but we thought that _____. |
| Wrap around | Ask students to write (or think about, for younger students) their ideas about a topic. In groups of four, they share their ideas, taking turns. Student A shares one idea, and then Students B, C, and D each share one idea. Each student must repeat the statement of the previous student before sharing his or her own. Repeat the process for each succeeding idea, sharing only one idea during each round. Continue in this way until all ideas are shared. | • If you anticipate that ELLs will only have one or two ideas to share, it may be advantageous to begin with those students so that they feel they have contributed a new idea, rather than simply repeating the same idea already shared.<br>• Students at very early levels of proficiency will benefit from hearing other students talk, so begin with more proficient students. | • I think that the story will be about _____.<br>• My first idea is _____.<br>• I have the same idea as _____.<br>I think the story will be about _____. |

# Bibliography

Adams-Byers, J., Whitseel, S. S., & Moon, S. W. (2004). Gifted students' perceptions of the academic and social/emotional effects of homogeneous and heterogeneous grouping. *Gifted Child Quarterly, 48*(1), 7–20.

Aronson, E. (2000). *Nobody left to hate: Teaching compassion after Columbine.* New York: W. H. Freeman.

Bakhtin, M. M. (1981). *The dialogic imagination: Four essays* (C. Emerson, Trans.). Austin: University of Texas Press.

Banks, J. A., Au, K. H., Ball, A. F., Bell, P., Gordon, E. W., Gutiérrez, K. D., Heath, S. B., Lee, C. D., Lee, Y., Mahiri, J., Nasir, N. S., Valdés, G., & Zhou, M. (2007). *Learning in and out of school in diverse environments: Life-long, life-wide, life-deep.* Seattle: University of Washington Center for Multicultural Education.

Barber, J. (2006). *The seeds of science/roots of reading inquiry framework.* Retrieved July 29, 2007, from http://seedsofscience.org/PDFs/InquiryCycle.pdf

Beck, I. L., McKeown, M. G., & Kucan, L. (2002). *Bring words to life: Robust vocabulary instruction.* New York: Guilford.

Bennett, N., & Cass, A. (1988). The effects of group composition on group interactive processes and pupil understanding. *British Educational Research Journal, 15*, 19–32.

Blachowicz, C. L. Z., & Fisher, P. (2000). Vocabulary instruction. In M. L. Kamil, P. B. Mosenthal, P. D. Pearson, & R. Barr (Eds.), *Handbook of reading research* (Vol. III, pp. 503–524). Mahwah, NJ: Lawrence Erlbaum Associates.

Bloom, B. S. (1956). *Taxonomy of educational objectives, handbook I: The cognitive domain.* New York: McKay.

Brinton, D., Snow, M., & Wesche, M. (1989). *Content-based second language instruction.* Boston: Heinle & Heinle.

Britton, J. (1983). Writing and the story of the world. In B. Kroll & E. Wells (Eds.), *Explorations in the development of writing, theory, research, and practice* (pp. 3–30). New York: Wiley.

Cazden, C. B. (1988). *Classroom discourse: The language of teaching and learning.* Portsmouth, NH: Heinemann.

Daoud, A. M., & Quiocho, A. M. L. (2005). I can't see you if I don't know you: How students create inequality. *Multicultural Perspectives, 7*(4), 3–12.

Davis, G. A. (2007). *Aphasiology: Disorders and clinical practice.* Boston: Allyn & Bacon.

Deci, E. L., & Ryan, R. M. (1985). *Intrinsic motivation and self-determination in human behavior.* London: Taylor & Francis.

DePaola, T. (1988). *Strega Nona: An old tale.* New York: Simon & Schuster.

Dewey, J. (1916). *Democracy and education: An introduction to the philosophy of education.* New York: Macmillan.

Dong, Y. R. (2004/2005). Getting at the content. *Educational Leadership, 62,* 14–19.

Durkin, D. (1978/1979). What classroom observation reveals about reading comprehension instruction. *Reading Research Quarterly, 14,* 481–533.

Education Department of Western Australia. (1996). *Oral language developmental continuum.* Melbourne: Addison Wesley Longman.

Elbaum, B. E., Schumm, J. S., & Vaughn, S. (1997). Urban middle elementary students' perceptions of grouping formats for reading instruction. *Elementary School Journal, 97,* 475–500.

Fernandez, C., Yoshida, M., & Stigler, J. W. (1992). Learning mathematics from classroom instruction: On relating lessons to students' interpretations. *Journal of the Learning Sciences, 2,* 333–365.

Fisher, D. (2005). The missing link: Standards, assessment, *and* instruction. *Voices from the Middle, 13*(2), 8–11.

Fisher, D., & Frey, N. (2007). *Checking for understanding: Formative assessments for your classroom.* Alexandria, VA: Association for Supervision and Curriculum Development.

Fisher, D., & Frey, N. (2008). *Better learning through structured teaching*. Alexandria, VA: Association for Supervision and Curriculum Development.

Flanders, N. (1970). *Analyzing teaching behavior*. Reading, MA: Addison-Wesley.

Flood, J., Lapp, D., Flood, S., & Nagel, G. (1992). Am I allowed to group? Using flexible patterns for effective instruction. *The Reading Teacher, 45*, 608–616.

Fung, I. Y. Y., Wilkinson, I. A. G., & Moore, D. W. (2003). L1-assisted reciprocal teaching to improve ESL students' comprehension of English expository text. *Learning and Instruction, 13*(1), 1–31.

Graff, G., & Birkenstein, C. (2006). *They say, I say: The moves that matter in academic writing*. New York: Norton.

Guan Eng Ho, D. (2005). Why do teachers ask the questions they ask? *RELC Journal, 36,* 297–310.

Halliday, M. A. K. (1975). *Learning how to mean: Explorations in the development of language*. New York: Elsevier.

Heath, S. B. (1993). Rethinking the sense of the past: The essay as legacy of the epigram. In L. Odell (Ed.), *Theory and practice in the teaching of writing: Rethinking the discipline* (pp. 105–131). Carbondale, IL: Southern Illinois University Press.

Heath, S. B. (1997). The essay in English: Readers and writers in dialogue. In M. Macovski (Ed.), *Dialogue and critical discourse: Language, culture, critical theory* (pp. 195–214). New York: Oxford University Press.

Hicks, D. (1995). Discourse, learning, and teaching. *Review of Research in Education, 21,* 49–95.

Hill, J. D., & Flynn, K. M. (2006). *Classroom instruction that works with English language learners*. Alexandria, VA: Association for Supervision and Curriculum Development.

Huxley, A. (1958). *Brave new world revisited*. London: Chatto & Windus.

Joos, M. (1967). *The five clocks*. New York: Harcourt, Brace, & World.

Justice, L. M. (2006). *Communication sciences and disorders: An introduction*. Upper Saddle River, NJ: Merrill/Prentice Hall.

Kagan, S. (1992). *Cooperative learning*. San Juan Capistrano, CA: Kagan Cooperative Learning.

Kantor, R., Green, J., Bradley, M., & Lin, L. (1992). The construction of schooled discourse repertoires: An interactional sociolinguistic perspective on learning to talk in preschool. *Linguistics and Education, 4*, 131–172.

Larson, K. (2006). *Hattie big sky.* New York: Delacorte.

Lingard, B., Hayes, D., & Mills, M. (2003). Teachers and productive pedagogies: Contextualising, conceptualising, utilising. *Pedagogy, Culture and Society, 11*, 399–424.

Lou, Y., Abrami, P. C., Spence, J. C., Paulsen, C., Chambers, B., & Apollonio, S. (1996). Within-class grouping: A meta-analysis. *Review of Educational Research, 66*, 423–458.

Mäntylä, T., Carelli, M. G., & Forman, H. (2007). Time monitoring and executive function in children and adults. *Journal of Experimental Child Psychology, 96*(1), 1–19.

Marzano, R. (2007). *The art and science of teaching: A comprehensive framework for effective instruction.* Alexandria, VA: Association for Supervision and Curriculum Development.

Marzano, R. J., Pickering, D. J., & Pollock, J. E. (2001). *Classroom instruction that works: Research-based strategies for increasing student achievement.* Alexandria, VA: Association for Supervision and Curriculum Development.

Michaels, S., O'Conner, C., Hall, M. W., & Resnick, L. (2002). *Accountable talk: Classroom conversation that works.* CD-ROM. Pittsburgh, PA: Institute for Learning.

Mutz, D. C. (2006). *Hearing the other side: Deliberative versus participatory democracy.* Cambridge, UK: Cambridge University Press.

Nystrand, M. (1997). *Opening dialogue: Understanding the dynamics of language and learning in the English classroom.* New York: Teachers College Press.

Nystrand, M., & Gamoran, A. (1991). Instructional discourse, student engagement, and literature achievement. *Research in the Teaching of English, 25*, 261–290.

O'Grady, W., Yamashita, Y., & Lee, S. (2005). A note on canonical word order. *Applied Linguistics, 26*, 453–458.

Oliver, R., Haig, Y., & Rochecouste, J. (2005). Communicative competence in oral language assessment. *Language and Education, 19*, 212–222.

Palincsar, A. M., Anderson, C., & David, Y. M. (1993). Pursuing scientific literacy in the middle grades through collaborative problem solving. *Elementary School Journal, 93,* 643–658.

Palincsar, A. M., & Brown, A. L. (1986). Interactive teaching to promote independent learning from text. *The Reading Teacher, 39,* 771–777.

Pianta, R. C., Belsky, J., Houts, R., & Morrison, F. (2007). Opportunities to learn in America's elementary classrooms. *Science, 315,* 1795–1796.

Resnick, L. (1995). From aptitude to effort: A new foundation for our schools. *Daedalus, 124*(4), 55–62.

Sachar, L. (1998). *Holes.* New York: Farrar, Straus, & Giroux.

Suárez-Oroczo, C., Suárez-Oroczo, M. M., & Todorova, I. (2008). *Learning in a new land: Immigrant students in American society.* Cambridge, MA: Harvard University Press.

Teachers of English to Speakers of Other Languages (TESOL). (2006). *PreK–12 English language proficiency standards: Augmentation of the World-Class Instructional Design and Assessment (WIDA) consortium English language proficiency standards.* Alexandria, VA: Author.

Tobin, K. (1987). The role of wait time in higher cognitive level learning. *Review of Educational Research, 57*(1), 69–95.

Wilkinson, A. (1965). *Spoken English.* University of Birmingham, UK: Educational Review.

Wineburg, S. S. (1991). On the reading of historical texts: Notes on the breach between school and academy. *American Educational Research Journal, 28,* 495–519.

Woolf, V. (1938). *Three Guineas.* New York: Harcourt Brace.

Vygotsky, L. S. (1962). *Thought and language* (E. Hanfmann & G. Vakar, trans.). Cambridge, MA: MIT Press.

Zwiers, J. (2007). Teacher practices and perspectives for developing academic language. *International Journal of Applied Linguistics, 17,* 93–116.

# Index

Note: page numbers in *italics* refer to figures, tables, and boxes.

# About the Authors

**Douglas Fisher** is a Professor of Language and Literacy Education in the Department of Teacher Education at San Diego State University (SDSU) and a classroom teacher at Health Sciences High and Middle College. He is the recipient of an International Reading Association Celebrate Literacy Award and the Farmer Award for excellence in writing from the National Council of Teachers of English, as well as a Christa McAuliffe Award for excellence in teacher education. He has published numerous articles on reading and literacy, differentiated instruction, and curriculum design as well as books, such as *Creating Literacy-Rich Schools for Adolescents* (with Gay Ivey), *Improving Adolescent Literacy: Strategies at Work* (with Nancy Frey), and *Teaching English Language Learners: A Differentiated Approach* (with Carol Rothenberg). He has taught a variety of courses in SDSU's teacher-credentialing program as well as graduate-level courses on English language development and literacy. An early intervention specialist and language development specialist, he has taught high school English, writing, and literacy development to public school students. He can be reached at dfisher@mail.sdsu.edu.

**Nancy Frey** is Professor of Literacy in the School of Teacher Education at San Diego State University and a classroom teacher at Health Sciences High and Middle College in San Diego. Before moving to San Diego, Nancy was a special education teacher in the Broward

County (FL) Public Schools, where she taught students at the elementary and middle school level. She later worked for the Florida Department of Education on a statewide project for supporting students with disabilities in general education curriculum. She is a recipient of the Christa McAuliffe Award for excellence in teacher education from the American Association of State Colleges and Universities, and she was a finalist for the International Reading Association's Outstanding Dissertation Award. Her research interests include reading and literacy, assessment, intervention, and curriculum design. She has published in *The Reading Teacher, Journal of Adolescent and Adult Literacy, Educational Leadership*, and several other journals. She has coauthored books on literacy such as *Improving Adolescent Literacy: Strategies at Work, Reading for Information in Elementary, Scaffolded Writing Instruction*, and *Checking for Understanding*. She teaches a variety of courses in SDSU's teacher-credentialing program on elementary and secondary reading instruction and literacy in content areas, classroom management, and supporting students with diverse learning needs. Nancy can be reached at nfrey@mail.sdsu.edu.

**Carol Rothenberg** is a staff developer in the area of literacy and English language learners. Providing support and guidance to teachers across content areas and grade levels, she coaches teachers in planning, assessing, and reflecting on instruction. She has worked with elementary and secondary schools throughout the San Diego Unified School District, training teachers and administrators on effective programs and instruction for English language learners. An experienced classroom teacher, Carol has taught bilingual special education, Spanish, and English to migrant workers. She has coauthored books on effective instruction for English language learners, including *Teaching English Language Learners: A Differentiated Approach* (with Douglas Fisher) and *Language Learners in the English Classroom* (with Douglas Fisher and Nancy Frey). She currently teaches classes for new teachers on effective instruction of English language learners. Carol can be reached at crothenberg@sandi.net.

# Related Resources: Content-Area Conversations

At the time of publication, the following ASCD resources were available (ASCD stock numbers appear in parentheses). For up-to-date information about ASCD resources, go to www.ascd.org.

## Books

*Building Academic Vocabulary: Teacher's Manual* by Robert J. Marzano and Debra J. Pickering (#105153S25)

*Classroom Instruction That Works: Research-Based Strategies for Increasing Student Achievement* by Robert J. Marzano, Debra J. Pickering, and Jane E. Pollock (#101010S25)

*Classroom Instruction That Works with English Language Learners* by Jane D. Hill and Kathleen M. Flynn (#106009S25)

## Mixed Media

*Educating Linguistically and Culturally Diverse Students* by Belinda Williams [professional inquiry kit] (#998060S25)

*Strategies for Success with English Language Learners* [action tool] (#706088S25)

## Videos and DVDs

*How to Get Started with English Language Learners* [one DVD] (#608032S25)

*Maximizing Learning for English Language Learners* [three videos] (#403326S25)

For more information on related resources: send e-mail to member@ascd.org; call 1-800-933-2723 or 703-578-9600, press 2; send a fax to 703-575-5400; or write to Information Services, ASCD, 1703 N. Beauregard St., Alexandria, VA 22311-1714 USA.